THE ULTIMATE UNIVERSITY ACADEMIC SKILLS GUIDE

UniAdmissions

Published by RAR Medical Services Limited

www.uniadmissions.co.uk

info@uniadmissions.co.uk

Tel: +44 (0) 208 068 0438

THE ULTIMATE UNIVERSITY ACADEMIC SKILLS GUIDE

CHARLOTTE LEE

UniAdmissions

ABOUT THE AUTHOR

Charlotte is a final year medical student at Green Templeton College University of Oxford. She previously completed an undergraduate degree (Medical Sciences, BA Hons) at Balliol College, University of Oxford.

Throughout her time at Oxford University, she earned a number of academic distinctions, awards, and scholarships. Charlotte has a broad range of teaching and research experience, including working as a tutor and mentor for medical students at Balliol and Green Templeton Colleges. She has authored multiple peer reviewed articles and been involved in research at a number of institutes, including the Hospital for Sick Children (Toronto), Division of Cardiovascular Medicine (University of Oxford), Nuffield Department of Clinical Neurosciences (University of Oxford), Sleep and Circadian Neuroscience Institute (University of Oxford), Oxford Transplant Centre, and the Centre of Evidence – Based Medicine (University of Oxford). She was a founding member of the first hospital-based coronavirus testing centre in the UK, and also contributed to several research studies during the coronavirus pandemic, including vaccination and coronavirus test validation.

Whilst at Oxford, she was heavily involved in University life, including serving as the Vice – President of Balliol Junior Common Room and representing Oxford as the coxswain of the Women's Lightweight Blue Boat (2020) and at several international events. She was elected to represent the University of Oxford at the British Medical Association Medical Schools' Council and helped form the first trans-health education course that was later adopted by medical schools nationally. Whilst studying at Green Templeton, she was employed as Junior Dean, a role that focussed on fostering academic success of students and wellbeing of students.

CONTENTS

INTRODUCTION

Congratulations on your decision to go to university! Whatever your background, navigating your way to a place at university is tough, so well done on your successful application!

This book introduces and offers guidance about every skill you will need at university, regardless of your course subject. This guidance intends to empower you to be able to make the most of every opportunity you find at university and prepare you for academic life in the UK. As such, this is a great book to read before you head off to university but also something you should pack in your bag to refer to throughout your time in higher education. Although you're only just starting out, we've also included some guidance at the end of this book about postgraduate life too!

Starting university is a really exciting time, but at some point, every student finds it a daunting prospect! There is also a lot of information packed into this small book, so it's key to remember that you are expected to develop these skills during your time at university, not just by finishing the book! If you ever feel overwhelmed, we've outlined several sources of support you will have at university, but remember, going to university doesn't necessarily mean you can't seek support from your existing network and people you trust!

Picking up this book is great preparation for a successful and fun time at whatever university you're heading to. Hopefully it will reassure you and help you prepare for what you should expect to come across as you start this next chapter of your life! University is a brilliant and beautiful place to learn about new things, meet interesting people from all different backgrounds, and grow as a person

Good luck and I hope you have a great time!

Charlotte

WHAT IS UNIVERSITY?

Most simply, university provides education at a post-school level. There are over 100 universities in the UK and 100s of subjects you could study, each offering a unique experience! There are two broad types of university courses, split into undergraduate and postgraduate courses. Undergraduate courses require school level qualifications to be eligible to apply, whereas postgraduate courses often require a university degree in order to apply. Most undergraduate courses will take 3-4 years to complete, with Medicine, Veterinary Science, and Dentistry lasting longer.

In the United Kingdom (UK), you choose the subject you want to focus on at the same time as you apply for the university. At some universities, it is possible to later change course, however this varies between universities and you may need to wait for the next academic year to join the course, or even re-apply to the university and course.

Whatever subject you have chosen to study, you will have to adapt and learn new ways to study and learn. Course curriculum can be delivered via

- Seminars: classes made up of one lecturer and a small group of students, typically 5 – 20 students.
- Lectures: typically, large classes with a lecturer delivering a presentation to the group, with time for questions at the end of the session.
- Tutorials: interactive sessions with a professor with up to 4 students. You may be asked to prepare some work in advance for these sessions
- Flipped learning: learning material is given to students before the class to complete. The session is used for questions and informal quizzes or activities to consolidate knowledge.

Some courses also may include other activities, for example, debates, peer presentations, field trips, and case studies. In addition to these more formal and structured sessions, you will also learn by self-study. There are a lot of different ways you can approach self – study, and part of being a university student is figuring out the best approach for you!

University is a place for you to develop not just academically, but also as a person beyond work! At the beginning of your first term, the university will host a 'Freshers' Fair', where all the university clubs and societies will have a stall. Here, you will be able to sign up to whatever activities you want to try. Joining university clubs and societies are a great way to meet new people and they often organise social events as part of the club activities. So be open to trying a few societies – you can always pick the club(s) that you want to continue to be a part of after a few weeks and drop the rest from your schedule.

UNIVERSITY CAMPUS

Universities are made up of faculty buildings, libraries, laboratories and other facilities including sports areas, cafes and canteens, and recreational areas. Most universities in the UK are campus based but a few have no campus and are spread across the city. Even with a campus-based university, it can be very difficult to navigate and find your way around! All universities in the UK hold a Freshers' Week, which is a week dedicated to settling in the first-year students – orientating them around campus, hosting social activities to introduce students to each other, and holding faculty orientation lectures. Some universities also offer an orientation day or week usually a few months before freshers' week, to help new students adjust to university life.

LIFE AS A UNIVERSITY STUDENT

During university, you can live in university owned accommodation or rent privately. Most 1st year students choose to live in university owned accommodation for the first year because it is a great way to meet fellow students. Often there are 6-10 students with individual bedrooms that share a kitchen and living facilities. There will be laundry facilities in the building too. University facilities like libraries and work rooms will often be close to the accommodation, which can be a bonus in the first year whilst you're getting used to the university town and living alone.

You may need a laptop for your university work and this can be a significant and costly purchase for some students. Shopping around to see the discounts different companies have for students can help with the cost but you should also contact your university to see if you are eligible for any financial support. There are also some good second-hand laptops available for purchase, but make sure you buy through a reputable seller to get a good functioning and reliable machine. There are computers available at all universities for students' use so you may choose to see how you go without one, but be aware that you may find you need one urgently so may not be able to get the best deal. Some students choose to purchase a printer as well, but every library will have a printer and photocopier available to use for a small charge and you may find that the university printing costs are lower than your own.

SAFETY AS A UNIVERSITY STUDENT

This book's main purpose is to help prepare and guide you through university academic life, but every book focussing on student life should include a few words on student safety. The UK is a relatively safe place, but university life is often a student's first experience of living alone and considering personal safety. This small section is for every student, regardless of race, gender, or sexual orientation. Unfortunately, other people's actions and choices can sometimes impact your safety or how safe you feel. This can lead you to second guess your actions or behaviour. It is important to not feel guilty or feel at fault for another person's behaviour or choices.

Although it shouldn't be up to you to ensure your safety from other people's actions (it should be up to them not to behave like that!) here we include a few tips to help empower you in any situation you may find yourself in. It is always safer to be with other people you trust, but you will find yourself on your own at some point during your university life - stay in well-lit and busy areas and consider getting a personal attack alarm from your student union. Often these are free of charge.

If something or someone worries you whilst you are out and about, go into a store and speak to someone about it, this could be a member of shop staff or even a person shopping. If you are on campus and worried, you can go into any university building and speak to staff. Additionally, there are often security spots that are well signposted where you can head to, which are well lit areas with a phone-line to the campus security service.

Make sure you have a phone number of a taxi company saved into your phone. The student union will often have a recommended taxi company to use (sometimes with a discount for students!) It's always useful to have it ready in your phone so you can get home quickly and safely. A few UK universities offer a free shuttle bus to and from campus or subsidise taxi journeys home if you are leaving campus late at night. Ask the student union or campus security if your university does this. It is always better to have some background knowledge about the different ways you can get home safely. That way, no matter what happens, you know what you can do to help yourself, whether that is getting some help from another person or using a taxi to get back home. More information can be found on your university's website.

HOW IS UNIVERSITY DIFFERENT FROM SCHOOL?

Here, we will focus on the academic differences between school and university. Most simply, university is academically more challenging than school work because it requires knowing concepts, applying them, and sometimes justifying your thought process. Other academic skills are also needed at university, like referencing, presentation skills, and critical appraisal. One academic once described university as a place that:

'teaches you how to think, not what to think'

This is different to school, which typically teaches you facts i.e. what to think rather than giving you the transferable skills to consider concepts and opinions.

FACILITIES AT UNIVERSITY

Your university will cater for hundreds or even thousands of students, and so will have a much larger campus than your school. Please note, some universities in the UK (primarily the universities based in London), will have a small main campus but will also have faculty buildings spread across the city. It is easy to underestimate the physical size of your university, but every student will get lost at least twice during their first week! Whilst you are finding your way around, make sure you leave enough time to navigate your way to classes and look up their locations before, to check where they are located!

Universities will offer more than buildings to work in, including: dedicated sports centres for students to use, catering services, seminar rooms, music practise rooms, meeting rooms, laboratories, and archives. Unlike at school, you won't be shown every single facility that the university offers and you may have to go looking for things yourself! The student union website is a good place to start, but often searching online for Your University Name and The Facility You Want, will give you the information you're looking for!

Key Point: Your university buildings will have lots of facilities for you to make use of, but students often have to be proactive to find them in order to use them!

YOUR UNIVERSITY PEERS

UK universities often have undergraduate students (students straight from school) and postgraduate students (students who have already achieved an undergraduate degree. Many students believe that this distinction provides a separation between school – leavers and older adults. However, in each degree, there is a huge range of student backgrounds, for example, some may take years out to work or travel and others may be returning to university education after having a family. This means that your classes won't just be filled with students from school, but older adults who will bring a plethora of life experience to your classroom!

In addition, your university class will contain students from all over the world. Your professors will also be of a global background. This makes discussions and classes much more interesting as a range of opinions and experiences will be offered. Try to take advantage of this by listening with an open mind and attempting to understand each individual's perspectives!

Each student in your class at university will have chosen to be there – they will have chosen the university and also chosen the course to study, as such, you will find that your classes are full of highly-motivated students. You'll have so much fun being in this environment because you'll be surrounded by people passionate about what they're studying! Some students notice that this environment changes the way they will naturally behave in class, for example, they may feel more encouraged to speak up and contribute, or they may feel a bit intimidated! Both reactions are natural and expected, so don't feel pressured to speak in class if you don't feel comfortable to.

Key Point: Your classmates and teachers at university will be from a global and diverse background. This means that they will bring a range of experiences and perspectives to your classroom!

LEARNING AT UNIVERSITY

University typically has over 100 students per undergraduate course, meaning your lectures will contain over 100 fellow students. Students will be from different socioeconomic and cultural backgrounds. This means that you will have a diverse range of thought processes and opinions in your class with you, which will enrich your experience. This simply isn't possible on the same scale in a class of 30-40 children at school. However, the increased numbers in your classes also means that you might feel a little lost and unnoticed in your lecture theatre. This is a completely normal adjustment process that all students go through as they transition from school to university life.

You may also find that there are fewer opportunities for individualised feedback at university compared to your school. At school, students receive feedback from their teachers in class and through written comments on their work. For undergraduate courses, university feedback often only comes by a raw score for submitted assignments. If your course includes a research project, then you will get more closely guided by your supervisor, who you can always ask for feedback.

> **Key Point:** University involves a lot of independent study and much less supervision than provided in a school environment.

TIME MANAGEMENT AT UNIVERSITY

At university you are responsible for your own work and motivation. This means that it can be very easy to fall behind if you don't focus enough on your academic life. You will be assigned an academic supervisor who may meet with you each term. This is probably the only person who will hold you to account for your academic performance and work, unlike school, where academic non-performance or class absences will be picked up very quickly by your teachers. As such, you really need to be self-motivated in your independent learning!

There is also less structure in your university student day compared to at school. School typically is structured per hour, with a set time to go home. At university, you may have only a couple of lectures per day or even entirely free weekdays. If you don't have a strong sense of motivation or the skills to work independently then this can be very difficult to adjust to. Equally, this can be difficult for students who work well independently as there is no 'home time', instead, students have to take responsibility for when they are going to stop working for the day. The decision to stop working requires a lot of maturity and self-awareness, so many students struggle with this when they transition to university. If you identify with this, a short-term strategy to help you adjust to university life, is to choose a time at which you will put down your laptop and work, no matter what you are doing. Lots of students choose 5pm to do this, but it may differ slightly if you have a different work schedule. We will cover how to approach independent work and time management in the How to Revise, Time Management, and How to Take Notes sections.

> **Key Point:** At university, you will be in charge of your own schedule and working hours – this can be really difficult, no matter how organised you are!

RELATIONSHIPS AND CUSTOMS AT UNIVERSITY

Because your university class will be much more diverse than your school, sometimes you will encounter different social situations, customs, and traditions. Friendships at university tend to have less traditional barriers like at school, for example, it's very normal for first year students can be friends with final year students. Generally, students at university are more open to all kinds of people and have the maturity to form friendships despite differences.

Some universities offer tutorials (for example, Oxford, Cambridge and Durham) where you will learn in very small groups from a professor. Often the professor teaches only your group of a few students for the entire year, and will invite your group to several social events, like dinners at your university or coffee. At school it is completely inappropriate for a teacher to issue these invitations to a student, but at university they are quite normal to receive as a group of students! It is important to remain professional at these events and remember that you are their student at all times. These social events often function as part of their mentoring and can allow you to network with other lecturers and professionals, meet other students, and be shown a different side to university life!

At university, there can be a lot of sporting traditions, for example, a varsity match. This is where women and men compete in a sport like rowing, rugby or swimming, against a 'rival' university. Traditional rivalries include Oxford and Cambridge, Newcastle and Durham, and King's College London and University College London. Unlike school, the majority of students will go to these varsity matches to support their university (even if they don't know anything about the particular sport!) and it is a huge social event. Often, old members of the university will come back to the city to attend the match too. Even if this doesn't sound like your cup of tea, you should try to go with your friends at least once to just experience the atmosphere – you won't ever get the opportunity to go as a student after you graduate!

Key Point: Friendships and working relationships can be different from what you have experienced at school. If you remember to be open minded and respectful, you can't go wrong!

SUPPORT AT UNIVERSITY

The transition to university can seem daunting to many students, but despite the higher expectation for independent work and motivation, there will be plenty of people who can guide you. You may be assigned a welfare supervisor who will check in with you every so often to see how you are doing. You may also be assigned a subject mentor, faculty supervisor, or student in a higher year who you can reach out to for help. These sources of support will contact you either before or soon after you start at university, so look out for their email. Lots of students forget what email they used to sign up for university mailing before they had a university issued email account, so make sure you check all of your inboxes!

In addition to your allocated advisers, you will also be able to access the university counselling services and healthcare services. In the UK, healthcare is provided by the National Health Service (NHS), and usually your General Practitioner (GP) is the best person to contact in a non-emergency situation.

MYTHS ABOUT LEARNING STYLES

There are lots of different myths regarding what makes a good student and a good learning session. This chapter will debunk some of these myths and hopefully empower you to study in the way that suits you!

MYTH 1: YOU ARE A 'TYPE' OF LEARNER

During school, you may have come across different ways of learning, for example, learning visually, through audition, or by doing activities. You may even have been told or completed a test that informed you were a certain type of learner. If you have been told you are a certain type of learner, this label is intended to tell you that you worked best through that specific type of learning. However, the categorisation of students into types of learners has been disproven. You may find you prefer to work in certain ways but this doesn't mean you are a type of learner – it's part of human nature to have preferred ways of doing any task. It is incorrect to put yourself into a box defining how you learn because methods of learning will be different depending on the type of information, your familiarity with the content, and difficulty of the information. As such, this chapter will cover different ways you can approach learning with the emphasis that 'types of learners' don't exist. Instead, you can use whatever learning approach is most suitable to the type of information!

Typically, if a student is assigned a 'learning type', they are told they are either a visual, auditory, kinaesthetic (doing something physically), or reading/writing preference. However, there are actually 5 learning approaches and as we said before, you may use all of them! Lots of students find they prefer some learning approaches over others and tend to use those more. However, using your less favourable learning approaches can help with information you're really struggling with – by changing your approach, you can revolutionise your understanding and learning. Here, we will go through each learning approach so you can tackle your work in multiple ways!

> **Key Point:** Labels like 'visual type of learner' are incorrect! There are multiple ways you can approach learning and you can utilise each approach throughout your time at university.

VISUAL APPROACH

Lots of students believe that visual learning is based on reading notes and textbooks, however, using a visual approach to learn primarily means using diagrams, images, or symbols to understand concepts. Every student during university will use this approach at some point. Diagrams and graphs are brilliant for condensing down information you are already familiar with and understand. The diagram then serves as a good memory prompt or even, in a written exam, it may be used as a figure within your written answers – this saves time and demonstrates your understanding!

Other visual approaches can involve pictures. These can be pictures you draw to literally represent facts and concepts, or images you associate with a topic. A common technique to use is to draw a picture based on the key part of the fact you're trying to remember – if you're trying to remember the name Mr Maraviroc, you could split the name into 'mara' and 'roc', and visually represent this as woman named Mara next to a rock. From recalling this image, you will then prompt your memory to the name: Mr Maraviroc.

AUDITORY APPROACH

An auditory approach involves any method that involves you listening to the information. To learn new content, auditory learning is best to use with short periods of concentration. Longer auditory resources are great to revise or to reinforce your learning. It's important to know your learning goal and then be able to use the right length and right type of auditory learning resource.

Most university students underutilise auditory approaches to learning because they believe it's ineffective due to their experiences with lectures. It is important to note that lectures are designed to explore content and usually last for at least 1 hour. This means that it's impossible for any student to remember every single word said during a lecture without notes to prompt you. Furthermore, it's also impossible to keep optimal focus for an entire lecture. As such, longer resources can be used in addition to other learning – either as an introduction to the topic that is later reinforced by book learning or used to consolidate existing learning.

As discussed above, you can use auditory approaches for short bursts of learning with high levels of concentration. Your university may supply short clips of mini-lectures, demonstrations, or summary videos. Alternatively, there are plenty of mini podcasts available from national societies or student run projects that are accredited information sources that are free to access. Many students use auditory approaches to learning at the end of their work day, because it's so different from any other learning approach. This allows students to refocus on work and stretch their brains to consolidate knowledge learned earlier or learn one more topic before calling it a day.

Longer podcasts or recorded lectures can be listened to effectively with mid – to high levels of concentration. Many students listen to these resources whilst travelling or doing other errands, allowing them to study no matter their schedule. As such, more and more students are utilising podcasts or recorded lectures as the main learning approach.

VERBAL APPROACH

Verbal approaches to learning can involve any technique involving speaking or writing. Most commonly, students using a verbal learning approach utilise word memory tricks like mnemonics or acronyms. Acronyms are discussed later in the How to Revise chapter. Mnemonics can be used to remember spellings, a sequence or hierarchy of a concept, or lists of information. An example is the mnemonic: 'my very easy method just shows us nine (planets)', which is a memory aid for the order of the planets: Mercury, Venus, Earth, Mars, Jupiter, Saturn, Uranus, Neptune (and Pluto).

Other verbal methods can involve making up lyrics full of information and singing them to a song you're familiar with. You can also just read content allowed, playing around with different accents and emphasising different words. This can be a really effective way of learning and understanding content!

Using verbal approaches to learning is a great way to prepare for any exam that will be spoken or practical, where you have to talk through your actions with an examiner. It allows you to learn the content in a verbal manner and is remembered in your brain as spoken information. Some students are able to convert learning using other approaches into fluent, spoken exam answers easily, but others who find this difficult can prefer to learn the content in the same mode that they will be examined on it!

KINAESTHETIC APPROACH

This learning approach incorporates your motor memory into learning academic concepts. As a child, you may remember using kinaesthetic approaches like an abacus to add numbers or figurines to tell a story. At university, you may find these particular methods less applicable, but the premise stays the same. One commonly used kinaesthetic learning technique involves students learning concepts by doing small projects on them, often audits, surveys, or experiments. These activities allow the student to have a task to anchor their knowledge to and serve as a memory prompt. The act of doing the project also consolidates the knowledge by embedding the concepts into actions you have completed.

It can be difficult to create relevant projects or tasks to learn through. Some students recommend using the power of associations alongside the kinaesthetic approach by touching different fabrics or objects whilst learning different topics. This way, you can remember touching and feeling a certain object, triggering your memory of the associated facts you were studying at the time!

CATEGORISATION APPROACH

Categorisation is great for information that can be broken down into lists or groups. This way of learning relies on logical organisation of information to compartmentalise facts and concepts. A great way to do this is to create flow charts of your information – that way, when you're recalling information, you just need to mentally travel down one isolated path rather than sift through all of your knowledge.

Categorisation is also a good learning approach when you're revising – if you're familiar with the content, you can revise by categorising information into lists, flow charts or mind maps. Make up questions to ask yourself: if you're a medical student, you may ask yourself what are all the causes of nausea? You would then work out categories: drug based, disease based, age based... English literature students may ask: what are all the characters in this novel that support the interpretation that the book is about hope? What characters don't support this interpretation? And then work from there.

Central to categorisation is finding a pattern or system to organise your information. This is possible with almost every concept or topic and is a great way to synthesize large amounts of information!

> **Key Point:** There are 5 main approaches to learning. Each approach may be more suitable to the content you are learning or the examination style used.

MYTH 2: YOU WORK BEST IF YOU WORK IN SILENCE

At school, students are often encouraged to work in complete silence. Lots of students leave school thinking that working in silence is the best environment possible for them to learn in and try to emulate this at university. In fact, you can work in a spectrum of environments from noisy to silent – there is no correct option! The most popular environment are libraries with low level, continuous background noise. Working in these environments is also a great way to prepare you for the noise levels whilst you are doing exams – any examination you do at university will be in complete silence, but don't underestimate the noise generated by about 100 students turning pages and writing!

You may find that you do prefer working in complete silence but be mindful that even in reading rooms and libraries that are designated to be silent work spaces, other students can make noise or even talk, leading to feelings of frustration, stress, and lack of productivity. Some students also find the background noise during examinations to be distracting. Consider wearing earplugs whilst you work or finding smaller library rooms to work in. This can prevent you from getting irritated by any noise you can't control!

> **Key Point:** Work in whatever noise environment enables you to work productively and minimises stress. This can be a silent room or a noisier café.

MYTH 3: YOU SHOULDN'T LISTEN TO MUSIC WHILST WORKING

Another myth that originates from school is that you should not listen to music whilst doing work. There is no conclusive evidence that shows you should or shouldn't listen to music whilst working, but it's important to consider a few things before putting on your headphones! Firstly, whilst you work, you're essentially training and preparing your brain for your exams. This means if you can't listen to music during your final exams, you should make sure you're used to working without music. Some students find this adjustment quite difficult so whilst you do your university work, make sure you can switch between the two noise environments comfortably.

It's also important to consider why you have music on – is it because you don't want to focus fully on your work? If this is true, take a moment to reflect if you're mentally ready to work and ask yourself if there is anything you can do to reset and refocus – take a break, change your working environment, or have a glass of water! Just make sure that listening to music isn't a self-inflicted distraction! If you choose to listen to music whilst working, we recommend you listen with a streaming service or using a playlist that is pre-prepared.

This means that you don't have to keep selecting songs, which can be very distracting!

> **Key Point:** Listen to music if you want to but make sure it's not a distraction!

MYTH 4: YOU SHOULD ALWAYS WORK INSIDE AT A DESK

The typical image of a student studying probably involves them working at some sort of desk and chair. But remember, you can work effectively outside, in an armchair, or even standing up! In fact, some students like to switch between working at a desk and another setting, as it provides a new environment and allows them to refocus on work. It is also good for your health as during periods with high work load (like during exam revision periods!) students can often spend hours inside without realising it. By working inside and outside, you are getting a healthy dose of fresh air and sunlight which is crucial for your mental and physical health. Whatever environment you choose to work in, make sure that you have access to all resources you need, for example, a computer and charging points. If you have chosen to work in a new place, it's important to reflect on how productive you were in that environment to help optimise your future work!

> **Key Point:** You can work wherever suits you! This might be in a library at a desk or in a green space outside.

HOW TO TAKE NOTES

Note taking is a skill you must master at university, regardless of what course you are taking and what exams you will have to sit. Notes can take many forms, but primarily function to capture conversations, lectures, seminars, or presentations so you can look back on them later. Notes are especially important for unique views or perspectives presented in your lectures that you will be unable to find anywhere else, or good explanations of difficult concepts that help you understand further. Most students choose to take notes even if they have a special learning plan that allows them to record all course content, or if the course content is uploaded to a central site for all students. This is because notes can condense information into your own words and the act of taking notes can help you understand and remember content. Furthermore, having the information written down and stored in one place helps to prepare you for exam season as you know that you can easily refer back to information rather than searching through hours of recordings.

> **Key Point:** Note taking is more than making a record of information. Instead, the process can help you organise your thoughts, helping you to remember the content.

THE PROCESS OF TAKING NOTES

There are many ways to take notes, each suited to different types of information and delivery. A common misconception many students have is that taking notes means writing down everything the lecturer is saying, almost word for word. This action is taking a transcript of the lecture, rather than taking notes! Notes can be copying down short phrases or words the lecturer uses, or also writing this information in your own words. Crucially, when you take notes you shouldn't be writing down a great quantity of words, but selectively using a few key words or a phrase to summarise what the lecturer is saying.

This is how taking notes can also help your understanding and recall of the content! Furthermore, many students say that taking notes keeps them engaged in the lecture as they have to actively consider and process the content that is being spoken, rather than watching the lecture like it is television! As such, you can think of effective note taking as a process with three steps that you must do in the following order:

1. Listening to the lecture
2. Processing the information – this may include condensing it down to a key word or phrase
3. Writing the note

If you miss out a step or complete the step out of order, then you are not taking good notes! Make sure that when you put pen to paper, you have listened to your professor and actively have understood what you are writing!

> **Key Point:** Note taking is more than making a record of information. Instead, the process can help you organise your thoughts, helping you to remember the content.

TYPES OF NOTES

There are two types of notes that you can make:

1. Notes that you will use in the future for essay planning or examination preparation
2. Notes that you have made to help you absorb and understand the information during the teaching session but won't use in the future

Your notes can fall into either or both categories, but unless you have made a note of a really important concept or useful table or diagram, you won't know what notes you have made until after your last course exams!

SETTING UP YOUR NOTES

The first step of taking notes is to have the equipment you need for your teaching session. Many students use laptops or paper to take notes, so use whatever is your personal preference! Sometimes life gets in the way of learning, so always keep a few pens at the bottom of your bag and a small notepad for days that you forget (or don't charge!) your kit. You'll also easily make friends in your lecture hall if you have a couple of spare pens to lend out!

This section will present a few options on how to take notes, but whatever strategy you choose, you must make sure your notes are labelled clearly with:

- Your name   You should include this even if you are using a laptop – it'll save you adding in your name to every note if you ever need to print them off!

- Date of lecture   This will help you align your notes with any online recordings. It'll also help future you if you are looking back on your notes for summer exams, or even exams in future years. The date can also help order your notes within a lecture series, which tend to build on previous lecture content.

- Lecture module title   Again, labelling with this will save future you a lot of time. The lecture module may be clear to you at the time, but you may not remember whilst you're revising.

- Lecturer name   Some students like to note down the lecturer's name so they can easily email them to ask questions, if necessary.

- Importance   Usually, if a lecture covers a topic that is a common exam question, the lecturer will help you out and tell you this! Write at the top of your notes something along the lines of 'common exam question' so you can easily identify it as a high-yield, important topic when you are revising!

> **Key Point:** Note taking is more than making a record of information. Instead, the process can help you organise your thoughts, helping you to remember the content.

NOTE TAKING METHOD 1: ANNOTATIONS

Arguably the most used method of note taking is annotation of lecture or seminar slides. At the beginning of a lecture, there may be a pile of printed out slides or you may have access to them via an online portal. These slides are a great resource to refer to, so if you don't have access to them, ask your lecturer or course administrator to alter this for future lectures.

A university lecturer will not read from their presentation slides, instead they will talk around the pictures or figures on each slide. This means that crucial information will probably not be written down and explained on your handout. To use the slides most effectively, you should turn to the slide the lecturer is using and annotate the diagrams or figures as the lecturer speaks with the information. If the slide only has written content, you may want to add a few words or a phrase as an adjunct to the text already there. Sometimes, you may find that you don't want to label the slide with more information and that's ok! What you write is up to you, but don't just write down every word the lecturer says, because this misses out the processing step of taking notes (step 2)!

Annotations can be useful for all types of lectures, but only if you annotate with useful information! Useful annotations could be explanations of calculations in science-based subjects, justifications for events or actions in socio-historic based courses, or technical terms in any subject. You may find annotations to be useful even if you use another note-taking strategy as your main approach, as you can annotate pictures, chunks of text, calculations, and even single words!

> **Key Point:** Annotating is a good method for students who struggle to listen and write at the same time, as the lecture slides provide a structure or framework for your notes to work off.

NOTE TAKING METHOD 2: THE BLANK PAGE

Another common method many students use to take notes is having a blank document or piece of paper and writing down key points. This is a brilliant way to ensure your understanding of the lecture content because there are no prompts or structure for you to conform your notes to, unlike with annotation. Writing notes this way truly ensures that you have processed what is being said and written it (usually) in your own words. If you choose to make notes this way, there is one key thing you must remember in order to make your notes useful. Many students forget that when they're in a lecture, the lecturer has built up context to their talk throughout their lecture. Many students write down a key point within a lecture, but fail to provide themselves with the context that the key point relies on to make sense! This means that when students review their notes, they have limited value in the future.

To prevent this, when you write a note, make sure you have an outline of the context that the point is based on. This might take the form of a small flow diagram at the top of your page, outlining the structure of the lecture (and therefore, the story of the lecture and context). Alternatively, you may choose to annotate your key point with a sentence of context that will jog your memory and understanding when you later review your notes. Whatever you choose to do, just remember that a key concept or interpretation means nothing if you don't understand or remember the context that forms its foundations.

If you choose to bullet point your notes, you also need to make sure they are well structured, so you can easily understand them when reviewing them later. Use headings, subheadings, highlighting, and different colours to create sections that are easily followed.

A blank piece of paper can be quite intimidating to tackle, so some students like to use mind-maps to take their lecture notes. The central node is the lecture concept or title, and each slide or concept introduced can be an offshoot from this central bubble. Mind-maps can be a great way to take notes as they visually organise the lecture onto one sheet whilst simultaneously forming the lecture context. However, some lectures can be difficult to mind-map, for example, physics and mathematics lectures, which are more suited to the blank page bullet point method detailed above.

Key Point: Using blank documents to write notes gives you flexibility in your note structure. This will enable you to take the correct learning approach (see Myths About Learning Styles) best suited to the session!

NOTE TAKING METHOD 3: THE CORNELL METHOD

This method is useful if you find it difficult to review your notes without a structure or particular task to complete. To use the Cornell Method, split your page into three sections:

Cue Section:

You should complete this section after the class. Here, you should write key points for the class and prompts to help you remember. You can also include vocabulary or technical words for the lecture.

Note Section:

This section is where you write any notes during your teaching session.

Summary Section:

This section should be completed after the class when you review your notes. Here, you should bullet point the main conclusions and learning points from the teaching session.

The Cornell Method is a great way to structure notes for any course, including maths and physics. This strategy can be especially useful whilst students are figuring out what makes a useful note, because you actively sift through and identify the key points from the lecture when you review your notes. This can help you learn what notes are valuable and slowly adapt your initial note taking.

> **Key Point:** The Cornell Method is a more structured way to take notes that can be useful for any course subject.

NOTE TAKING METHOD 4: TABLES AND DIAGRAMS

Many students forget that taking notes isn't limited to written notes, but can also include using diagrams and tables to condense information. Teaching sessions are delivered by experts in the field, so often their tables or diagrams are brilliant representations of information. If you copy down their figures, make sure you alter them and credit the source if you use them in your own academic work! Figures can be a brilliant way to process information, and remember, you can also annotate diagrams and tables with additional information to help you understand them!

NOTE AFTER-CARE

So, you've created some notes from a lecture and don't know what to do with them now. Firstly, you need to keep yourself organised so you can easily find your notes when you need them. Imagine yourself in the future, around your exam time, super stressed and needing to find a particular quote from your lecturer that you vaguely remember exists but crucially don't know the exact wording they used. The last thing you want to have to do is search through a boxful of loose pieces of paper for a single line of writing! If you have paper notes, use binders and file dividers to clearly separate your notes into categories (usually lecture modules or examinations). Some students even have a piece of paper at the front of every section and write the lecture title and 'page number' to form an informal contents table at the start of each section to help them locate notes quickly. If you don't want to buy files or binders, you can use string or ribbon to keep your notes together.

After you have organised your notes, keep them in a designated place that is safe and dry. Your paper notes will be the only copy you have, so keep them safe! This means you shouldn't pile them underneath a window (in case rain water ruins them) or underneath your desk (where a cup of tea could fall on them) …

If you have digital notes, make sure they are backed up somewhere. Either use a virtual or old-style hard-drive to keep a copy, just in case the unthinkable happens to your computer!

> **Key Point:** Good organisation of notes is almost as important as the note quality – your notes are useless if you can't find them!

REFERRING BACK TO YOUR NOTES

Regardless of the note category you think you have (please see 'types of note' section above), you should always review your notes after you make them. Most students aim to read through their lecture notes approximately 3 – 5 days after the lecture. This gives a spaced repeat of the information which helps to consolidate your knowledge and improves your recall. This is similar to the spaced repetition that underlies revision – please see the How to Revise Chapter for more information. There are many ways to review notes:

- Some students re-write their notes when reviewing them, making them neater and adding information from wider reading or other complimenting lectures.
- Some students go through their notes and highlight any key points
- Some students write summaries of their notes on small flashcards that can help remind them of the key conclusions of the lecture.
- Some students use the Cornell note taking method (please see above section).
- Some students just read through their notes to review them, potentially adding a few annotations.

Online recordings of teaching sessions are becoming increasingly available and commonly students ask if they should review their lecture notes and listen to the lecture again at the same time. Unfortunately, there is no clear answer or formula, but you should consider that doing this will literally double your work load, which is a significant increase. Given this and the length of lectures, students should only re-listen to lectures at a slower pace than they are delivered. For example, if you have 2 hours of lectures each day, you should re-listen and review your notes for one lecture per day or every two days. This is to prevent burnout and also maximise the efficiency of each review session. If you don't want to re-listen to every single lecture again, many students will re-listen and review the more important or 'high – yield' lectures, for example, lectures that cover common exam questions or introduce complex concepts. Whatever your strategy is, make sure that it is a sustainable and beneficial pace.

> **Key Point:** Try to look over your lecture notes a short while after hearing the lecture. This will refresh your memory and help consolidate your knowledge.

HOW LONG SHOULD I KEEP MY NOTES FOR?

After your exams, you may feel the urge to cleanse your space of all of your academic work. You are not alone, but try to resist recycling (or burning!) all of your notes and revision work! One of the most annoying and frustrating problems you can have as a student is knowing that you once had a useful note or resource for your work or exam and not being to find it (or knowing that you got rid of it in the past!) Although it can be annoying to move in and out of student accommodation, but try to keep at least the notes you have actively used over the past year (category 1 notes, please see above section). Students studying Dentistry, Veterinary Sciences and Medicine should keep every year's notes in a safe place, as they can be very useful to refer to over the years, especially for final year exams. These notes do take up precious shelf space in student accommodation but having your valuable notes when you need them is a small price to pay in exchange for the indescribable frustration of knowing you had vital notes on a topic and threw them away!

EFFECTIVE COMMUNICATION

Throughout your life, you will need to communicate to other people — whether this is with your lecturer, peers you work with, or your friends! It is essential that you can communicate well so your perspective can be understood and so that you can appreciate other people's points of view. Good verbal communication involves a well-formed piece of information that is conveyed to someone else who is actively listening for this information. Verbal communication is complimented by non-verbal communication, like body language and facial expressions.

During university, your ability to communicate well will sometimes be assessed formally, through presentations or debates. Chapters that cover how to give good presentations and debates come later in this book! But beyond formally assessed communication, having good communication skills will also enable you to take full advantage of interactions with your supervisors or professors. It is crucial to formulate a good working relationship with any supervisor, especially if you are undertaking an assessed research project or dissertation. You will have limited one-on-one time with your supervisor and potentially only one-off chances to speak with visiting experts or advisers. As such, it is a huge benefit to communicate a clear vision of your project or communicate what you're struggling with, and get valuable feedback. Central to a good working relationship is mutual understanding - good communication facilitates this!

It is important to note that you will come across people who may have difficulties communicating and interacting with others. You may have some of these difficulties yourself. As such, regardless of who you are talking to and what information you are communicating, there must be a foundation of respect and patience onto which you build any conversation.

> **Key Point:** Good verbal communication requires both a speaker and a listener. Both parts are key to facilitate understanding.

NON-VERBAL COMMUNICATION

Non-verbal communication encompasses any message that a speaker may give without talking, for example, facial expressions, body language, or gestures. Non-verbal communication also includes 'vocalic' or 'paralanguage', which refers to parts of a verbal communication that doesn't contain words, like hesitation noises, pitch or volume. You may pick up on these non-verbal cues with little effort, but it might not come naturally to you.

Non-verbal communication can take on five roles in a conversation:

1. Reinforcement: the non-verbal cues could agree with the verbal message
2. Contradiction: the non-verbal cues could disagree with the verbal message. This could indicate that the speaker doesn't fully endorse the words they are saying
3. Substitution: a non-verbal cue could take the place in the place of a verbal message, for example, a facial expression!
4. Complementary: the non-verbal cues could agree with the verbal message and strengthens the message's meaning/impact
5. Accentuation: the non-verbal cues could accent or emphasise the verbal message, for example, banging on the table to help convey your passion and highlight your message

APPROACHING NON-VERBAL COMMUNICATION

Non – verbal communication can be complex to untangle, especially if it is contradicting the verbal communication. Here we have provided a basic approach to interpreting non-verbal which you can use as a foundation to develop your communication skills.

1. Face	Begin at the speaker's face – what is the speaker's facial expression like? Are they smiling or frowning? Are they making good eye contact with you?
2. Body	Closed off body language (crossed limbs or the speaker's body pointing away from you) might indicate that the person is defensive or unhappy about the message they are verbally delivering. If the speaker's body is orientated towards you and they are making good eye contact, then their body language is signalling that they are open to the conversation and your response.
3. Hands	After evaluating the speaker's facial expressions and body language, you can reflect on the speaker's gestures, for example, if they are using a lot of hand gestures then they may be conveying that they are passionate about the subject.
4. Paralanguage	Lastly, reflect on how the speaker is talking, for example, if they are talking quickly then they may be stressed or feeling a sense of urgency. Whereas they are speaking slowly, they may be mulling over their message content.

Key Point: Non-verbal communication can enrich any verbal message but can be difficult to interpret correctly.

ACTIVE LISTENING

Active listening is a crucial skill to develop during university. Developing this skill will help you in lectures and seminars, but it is so crucial for any professional relationship you have at university, for example during project work or industrial days. Active listening means listening to the words a person is saying but also the overall, complete message being communicated through non-verbal signals. Active listening is made up of several steps which should be completed in the order set out below:

1. The first step of active listening is to signal that you are listening. You can do this with your body language: making eye contact with the speaker, leaning forward to demonstrate your engagement, and by keeping your body language open to the speaker.

2. The second step is comprehension (shared meaning between the listener and the speaker). Comprehension can be approached using a bottom – to – top method or a top – to – bottom strategy. If you approach comprehension from a top – to – bottom method then you will prepare yourself for what the message is likely going to be. Then, you listen to the message and attempt to alter your expectations to match the message you are listening to, by organising the message into action points or concepts. Lastly, when you listen top – to – bottom, it is important to listen for any shifts in topic or summaries of what is said. Essentially, a top – to – bottom listening approach involves generating and maintaining an overview of the speaker's message. If you use a bottom – up listening approach, you need to be attentive to words that are emphasized by the speaker and to any repeated content. By doing this, you can take cues from the conversation to formulate the message.

3. The next step of active listening is retaining the information. Retention of what is being communicated is key because this enables you to extract meaning from the message. Retention also enables you to place what you are hearing into context, either within the conversation or within a greater setting.

4. After you have comprehended and retained the speaker's message, you should respond to the speaker. There are three ways you can respond: You can put the speaker's message into your own words and read it back to the – this can be a very effective way of checking comprehension and interpretation of the speaker's message. You could also ask questions to clarify their meaning. Lastly, you can offer the speaker a concise overview of the main points and the overall meaning of the message. This way, the speaker and the listener can be reassured that the message has been correctly communicated.

5. Lastly, you can formulate your response to the speaker's message. This is dependent on the content of the message – it may be confirming an action point you will carry out or it may be your opinion! Make sure your response has addressed all of the key points the speaker has raised.

It is important to notice the speaker's body language whilst they are communicating as it may add context and provide a hidden meaning to their spoken message. If you want more information about interpreting body language, we have covered the topic earlier in this chapter. Additionally, whilst you are practising active listening, you should always remember not to form judgements about the message the speaker is communicating. It is crucial to approach listening with an open mind! You will notice that in the steps above, it is only at step 5 that you start to think about your reaction to the message - you should always try to resist formulating your own reaction or message to the speaker until the speaker has finished communicating. If you formulate your return message before the speaker has finished communicating, you are using only a portion of the message to form an interpretation of the speaker's meaning – this can cause you to miss crucial information.

> **Key Point:** The steps of active listening are: signalling your attention, comprehending the message, retaining the message, responding to the message, and lastly providing a return message if applicable.

STRUCTURING ACADEMIC DISCUSSION

Academic discussion is a distinct type of conversation or communication that focuses on one topic or question. At university, you will encounter four types of academic discussions:

- Informal discussions in classroom settings
- Written academic discussions in work assignments, usually of concepts or discussions
- Formal debates (these are discussed in the Debating Skills chapter and so will not be detailed here).
- Written academic research discussion (these aren't really discussions like the types above, please see the Publication chapter for guidance on research discussions).

Many students believe that academic discussion must be filled with really impressive sounding pronouncements and quotes. This is completely incorrect and don't let that misconception intimidate you or hold you back from getting involved! Academic discussions are a place where you can critically think about information (please see the Critical Thinking chapter), and hear multiple perspectives and opinions about a topic. They can involve using information, quotes, or personal experiences to support your points of view, but are informal places of discussion. Academic discussions can involve disagreements and differences of opinion, but these disagreements must remain respectful and relevant to the topic. There are three main pillars to any academic discussion, and it can be very helpful to remind participants of these principles before the conversation starts (or as close to the start as possible!):

Having respect for all discussion participant despite difference in viewpoints

Foundations of a

Productive Academic

Discussion

A non-judgemental and safe zone for discussion

A clearly defined topic of discussion

Key Point: Academic discussions should be a safe zone for students to discuss academic concepts and learn other viewpoints.

MAINTAINING RESPECT IN INFORMAL DISCUSSIONS

Some academic discussions may be led or moderated by your lecturers or teachers. This can help to maintain the topic of conversation and give a rough guide or structure to the students. Other conversations may not be moderated officially and each participant should share moderation duties, by speaking if they find the conversation off-topic. Academic discussions are a somewhat artificial environment where you can disagree and debate things with your coursemates and then leave the class as friends! Free speech at university is a well debated topic and you may even come across free speech related dilemmas at university, yourself.

We don't presume that this guide could fully address this dilemma, as each situation can be unique and often can provoke intense emotions or reactions from discussion participants and beyond. Whatever your opinion on free speech is, you must remember that academic discussions should have humanity, respect, and empathy. Academic discussions can sometimes involve personal contributions, and even if a discussion participant (or indeed yourself!) disagrees with the point, they shouldn't disagree with the person contributing it, on a personal level. It can be difficult to moderate other participants but it can get easier with more practice! Some useful phrases that can help moderate academic discussions and maintain the discussion safe space include:

- Thank you for your contribution to this discussion, may I remind everyone that we are discussing ... and the core principles of this discussion include respecting each discussion participant
- Thank you for your point but I think your statement about ... was a bit personally orientated – would anyone like to respond to that or we can move on from that point...
- I disagree with your point but your explanation helps me to appreciate where you potentially are coming from.
- I completely disagree with what you have just said there. This academic discussion isn't a place for us to abandon our morals and humanity but I don't want to abandon this discussion or start an argument, so I would like to move on from your point if that's ok with everyone
- I'm not sure that this a productive avenue for us to discuss, let's return to the main principle we are discussing here...
- Given my personal experience with this topic, I believe really strongly about... but I appreciate that my personal experience is the main reason I believe this and other people's experiences might be different.

You can see with the examples above, you can be quite forceful with your words, whilst being constructive. Even if you strongly disagree with someone's point, you shouldn't break the foundations of an academic discussion. Many students find it difficult to verbalise their discomfort during some conversations. Although university is a place of diversity and equality, in some discussions, you may feel a power dynamic or imbalance between participants.

If you don't feel comfortable sharing how you feel or your perspective, you can always speak to a moderator or a course administrator to seek support and address the issue.

> Key Point: It can be difficult to voice your opinion or disagree with discussion participants. Don't feel pressure to speak out if you don't want to – you can always address it after by speaking to someone you trust.

WRITTEN ACADEMIC DISCUSSIONS IN WORK ASSIGNMENTS

Some written work assignments may require you to form an academic discussion within your work and reach a conclusion. It can be really difficult to approach this, so this section will help guide you through writing an academic discussion for a work assignment.

Generally, a written academic discussion should have balance. This means that both sides of the argument should be presented. To structure your argument, you should present all of the evidence on one side or perspective, and then present the evidence on the others. Some students are taught at school to alternate between for and against paragraphs in their work, but this can be a more confusing and weaker structure. Remember, structure can influence the strength of your arguments, so make sure it's clear for the reader to follow. It can be helpful to signpost your work with phrases like:

- In favour of the statement…
- Supporting this argument…
- However, in contrast…
- Contradicting this….

True balance strictly requires equal weighting, but don't sacrifice quality of your writing by forcing more or fewer words, to make the paragraphs equal lengths! Creating a false sense of balance by adding in space-filling sentences can weaken your arguments. It is better to either be satisfied with your natural writing and balance, or think up another point to even out the amount of discussion you are giving to each side!

Although it is important to provide a balanced view in academic writing, in some types of writing, it may be suitable to be slightly biased in your writing, and present one argument more strongly than the opposing view. This can depend on the essay question, your professor's personal preference, and the type of work assignment – for example, an academic opinion piece can present an 'unbalanced' view. Here, it is always good practice to acknowledge the other side of an argument, even with just a single paragraph that is clearly signposted as an appreciation of another perspective.

Once both sides have been presented, regardless of the 'balance' you have chosen to provide in your writing, most students struggle with what to do with the opposing views in their essays. Lots of students are taught for school exams to write 'I believe this argument is stronger because', but this is something that you should avoid writing, as a university student. This is because it is not evidence based and also states an undefined relative comparison of 'stronger or weaker'. Instead, you should refute the opposing argument by using evidence-based rationale, for example:

- However, it is now known that Churchill had seen reliable intelligence of the German tank design, therefore, it is more likely this act was a feint to mislead the opposition.
- However, given the presence of a rash, the symptoms presented indicate that Kawasaki disease was the underlying pathology.

Key Point: Make sure you have a clear and signposted structure when presenting academic discussions in written form.

HOW TO REVISE

This chapter will take you through the entire process of preparing for your exams. We'll start at the beginning and work through planning your revision, revision techniques and tips, and finish with receiving results! Revision is different from routine university work. It often requires both memorisation of a large amount of information and application of this knowledge. Furthermore, many (if not all!) students can feel more stressed about the looming examination days than normal university work submission deadlines. As such, you might find your revision period to be a stressful period, especially as exams draw closer. With the tips and techniques in this section, hopefully you will feel academically prepared and also emotionally ready to face exams!

GOAL SETTING

Before you start revising, you must decide what your goals are for your upcoming exam(s). Your aim could be to pass an exam or do really well and get a prize from your faculty. Whatever your goals are for the upcoming exam(s), make them SMART:

- **S**pecific: what are you going to accomplish? Why? When will this happen? What does achieving this goal mean?
- **M**easurable: how can you tell that you are successful in achieving this goal?
- **A**ttainable (achievable): can you achieve this goal?
- **R**elevant: is this goal realistic? Can you commit to it?
- **T**ime-bound: what is your start and finish date?

By writing out your goal(s), it will give you a specific focus as you plan your revision and you can always return to them to top-up your motivation whilst revising. An example goal could be:

'In my anatomy exam in 50 days, I will achieve at least 65%'

This goal is a SMART goal because it is specific and clear, with a measurable way of determining success. There is a time limit and the goal is relevant and reasonable.

WHEN YOU SHOULD START REVISING

Whenever your exams fall in the school year, you will always feel like there just isn't enough time to fit in all of your work and revision. Some students believe that starting revision earlier is always better, but you need to be cautious about burning out. The time approaching exams can be very stressful and revising for a long period of time can give you mental fatigue, negatively affecting your exam performance. As such, it is important to time your revision and structure your time so your exam performance peaks at the same time that your exams are scheduled. This is very similar to training for a marathon or high-level sports – their training programme is designed so that the athletes are in peak physical performance during their competition. Generally, if you revise for 5 days a week, a good time to sit down and start revising is about 5 – 6 weeks before your exams begin. If you have a part-time job or other responsibilities whilst studying, you may want to begin about 8 weeks before your exams begin to ensure you cover all of the material. It is not the best idea to start revising too late, forcing yourself to 'cram'. 'Cramming' refers to a short and intense period of time during which you try to revise for an exam or test. 'Cramming' generally results in knowledge being logged in your very short-term memory and poor exam results.

Ideally, you will plan your revision and begin studying well before the exam, however, we recognise that sometimes this isn't possible due to life events or changes of circumstance. If you find yourself with a very short amount of time to revise, you must discuss this with your academic adviser about your options for taking this exam. You may be able to postpone your sitting or apply for mitigating circumstances to be considered. Having enquired about this, you must still try to prepare for the exam as it is unlikely that you will get an immediate answer from the examiners. Have a look at the section 'familiarise yourself with the exam content' and focus on anything you deem to be a 'high yield topic' (discussed below). You must aim to study for as many marks as you can during the shortest amount of time possible.

It may feel counterproductive to take time to relax and unwind, but this time can be highly stressful – make sure you look after yourself!

> **Key Point:** If possible, start revising about 5 – 6 weeks before the exam to maximise exam performance whilst preventing burn out.

FAMILIARISE YOURSELF WITH THE EXAM STYLE

Now you have set your goals, the next step is to make sure you know what exam you're revising for. This sounds very basic but it is the most common step students miss, leading to underperformance in exams. The best way to make sure your revision will be exam relevant, is to look up all past papers you have access to. There may be 2 types of papers available:

1. Recent papers that are just like the exam you will sit
2. historic papers that have either
   a. different content and the same style
   b. the same content but a different exam style.

Make note of what exam papers are type 1 or type 2 (above). Next, download all the past papers you have access to – this means that you will have guaranteed access to the papers if the university removes them for any reason or if there are technical issues. Read through at least 50% of the papers that conform to your upcoming exam (type 1). Keep the 'outdated' papers (type 2) for later. I recommend you don't open some of the papers so you can use them to give yourself a mock exam later.

Whilst you read through the papers, the first thing you should note is the exam structure. Write out a rubric of your exam – how much time you have overall and how many questions in each section and their style:

Section	Question	Type of question
1	1-5	Short answer, 1-3 sentences
2	1	Essay – write 1 essay from 3 title options
3	1	Essay – write 1 essay from 2 title options

TYPES OF EXAM QUESTION

- Multiple choice: these questions will give you options to pick the right answer from. Here, there will be a clear correct answer in the group of options. The best way to tackle these questions are to cover the options you are given and try to think of the right answer. Uncover and see if your answer is there – if it is, congratulations! If it's not, try to rule out answers and find the correct option by elimination.
Some students second guess themselves when they go to check their answers and end up changing them from correct options. To see if you're one of these students, mark your paper with your 'original pick' and your 'checked pick'. If you lose marks when you check your answers, consider not going back through the test – you may even decide to leave the exam early to resist changing your answers.

- Single best answer: Many students don't realise that these questions are different from multiple choice. Here, the question will provide you with several options to pick the best answer from. The options will contain several correct answers, but you must pick the best option from the bunch. These questions can be surprisingly tricky because the distinction between correct and incorrect is less clear than with multiple choice questions. The best way to answer these questions is to practise this style of question, ideally with practise questions and past papers. Additionally, you must read the question very carefully. Identify the key information within the question and if necessary, highlight it. See what answer meets what the question is hinting at!

- Essay questions: These questions are long and can be stressful as they often carry the most marks in an exam paper. When you answer these questions, make sure you have spent time to plan out your answer. Remember, you don't have to write the essay in the order that you read it in – a trick is to write your introduction last, when you have a good overview of what you have written in your essay and have reached your conclusions. This means that you can write a clear introduction that can give the shape to your essay and be a tight summary of your essay. Just ensure you leave enough room on the paper to insert your introduction at the end!

- Short answer: Short answer questions can have a range of marks attached to them. You should use the marks per question to guide how long your answer should be – in some exams a short answer question could expect at least 3 developed points in your answer but in others a couple of sentences is enough to gain the marks. Here, it's especially important to be familiar with past papers and know what your examiner is looking for. Regardless of the marks attached to these questions, the key thing you need to remember is to keep your answer focussed and to the point!

- Computational questions: These questions dominate science based subject exams, for example, maths and physics. Ensure you demonstrate your entire workings and though process – many students have shed marks on each question by writing 'QED' or 'assuming $x = y$....' without justifying it with workings out. These little marks lost all add up and could change your overall grade. Be meticulous and accurate with the answers you provide!

Next, figure out how many marks are available for each question. Lastly, calculate how much time you should roughly spend on each section: take the total exam time in minutes and divide it by the total number of marks available. In the example below, there are 122 marks and 120 minutes.

$$\frac{120}{122} = 0.98 \ ... of \ a \ minute \ for \ each \ mark$$

$$0.98 \times 60 = 59 \ seconds \ per \ mark$$

Please note, this only gives you a rough guide on how long to spend per mark and question. You may want to add in time to check your answers at the end. As you revise and get used to the exam style, you may find you need to allocate time differently, to spend longer on one question style and less time on another. However, this is a good technique to get you started!

At the end of these calculations, your rubric should look something like this:

Exam title: Paper 1, Female composers 1500-1800

Time: 2 hours

Section	Question	Type of question	Marks	Time to spend
1	1-5	Short answer, 1-3 sentences	Q1 = 2 Q2-5 = 5 Total = 22 marks	59 × 22 = 1298 *seconds* which is roughly 21 minutes
2	1	Essay – write 1 essay from 3 title options	50	59 × 50 = 2950 *seconds* Which is roughly 49 minutes
3	1	Essay – write 1 essay from 2 title	50	59 × 50 = 2950 *seconds* Which is roughly 49 minutes

If you want to leave time to check your answers at the end, decide how much checking time you want. Then take this time away from the overall total exam time. Use the remaining time. If we continue the example from above, if you want 20 minutes to check your answers, then:

$$120 - 20 = 100 \; minutes$$

$$\frac{100}{122} = 0.82 \; ...of \; a \; minute \; for \; each \; mark$$

$$0.82 \times 60 = 49 \; seconds \; per \; mark$$

Key Point: It is crucial that you have a clear idea of what exam you will be taking and how long per mark you have for each question!

FAMILIARISE YOURSELF WITH THE EXAM CONTENT

Now you know how you will be tested; the next step is to know what you'll be tested on. This is usually your entire curriculum but it can be sections of it, or even just stated as 'this year's work'. We'll take the example of being tested on the entire curriculum because it's the most common situation, but the following example steps can be used for any exam content. The first thing you need to do is download your course curriculum to give yourself guaranteed access to it. Try and make it into an editable file so you can cross things off and mark it as you revise.

The next step is the most important to get right – you need to identify the 'high yield topics. These topics are the course content items that frequently come up in exams. To identify these topics, make a list of each topic asked about per past paper question. You then might see that in 2015 and 2018, the exam focussed on the same or similar content, or other patterns like this. You should make a list of topics that have come up before, organised by most frequently asked down to asked one time previously. These are the topics that you need to prioritise and dedicate a good chunk of your time to studying.

In addition to the list, you can highlight these a certain colour on your curriculum list to make sure you don't miss any high yield topics. After you have done this, you need to look at the rest of the syllabus and identify topics that are the most next likely to come up in your exam. These topics might be related to 'high yield topics' or they could be topics the lecturers have particularly focussed on during term. These topics have less priority than the 'high yield topics', but still give them some attention during your revision period! Lastly, make a list of topics that have the least relevance to your exams – these might be topics too small to ask an essay question on or may be topics that are very niche and difficult to write an essay question for. You should still revise these topics, but this list organises content into priority order, meaning that you focus on the topics that are most likely to appear in your exams!

> **Key Point**: Make sure you take time and due diligence when making these priority lists as they are the foundation of your revision plan.

If you don't have any past papers to revise from, focus on what the lecturers have dedicated the majority of time on, think about what exam questions could be asked from your content, and ask other students from previous years about what the exam is like. Be careful when asking, you don't want to cheat but you may ask previous students for a more general idea about what the exam is like.

> **Key Point:** It is important to have a clear vision of the content that the exam will be testing you on.

COLLECT YOUR MATERIALS

You're going to need resources beyond past exam papers to put yourself in the best position to achieve your goals. Get out your notes from the year and take a few moments to make sure they're organised and easy to access – put all of your relevant notes together per topic and label them clearly! Next, look to see what books you may need over the coming weeks. You may have a reading list or recommended textbooks from your lecturers – use them, they've been recommended for a reason! For most books you can order them online for pickup at the library, enabling you to do one trip to the resource library and have everything you need to get a good start. Set a calendar reminder or alarm for the day the books are all due back at the library, so that you can return or renew them on time to avoid any fines!

> **Key Point**: Collate as many resources you think you may use during revision – it's always good to have these to hand, so you don't have to interrupt your revision schedule by going to the library in search of books!

PLANNING YOUR REVISION

After you have a clear idea of what you need to revise and collected all the resources you will need over the upcoming revision period, you now need to allocate your revision time. This process is remarkably similar to making a timetable for general work-related time management (see Time Management Chapter), however there are a couple of extra things you need to consider when making your timetable.

Firstly, repetition is key during revision so you need to schedule time to review and test yourself on knowledge you learned previously, throughout your entire revision period. There is a most ideal number of times you revise a topic and when you repeat a topic. This is called spaced repetition. Memory gets stronger the more they are retrieved (i.e. repeated), and science has shown that the best time to repeat them is just before you forget them. So, if you learn a new fact, you should test yourself and revise it a few minutes later, then a few hours, then a day, and then a few days later. This means you need to keep careful track of what topics you've revised and when you need to look over them again. It is easiest if you put all of these repeats in your timetable to start with, set out an hour a day to repeat topics, and stick to your plan!

> **Key Point:** Repetition is better than forgetting and then relearning facts that you revised a long time ago. Continually repeating topics means that you never forget and the information gets stored in your long-term memory.

Whilst you are planning your revision schedule, you should also plan for the 'worst case scenario'. This means you should plan catch up time just in case you fall behind with work and give yourself extra time to review any concepts you are struggling with. You're not planning to 'fail' at your schedule, but instead you're providing yourself with a built-in mechanism to help you succeed if you are struggling – it's a safety catch designed to prevent you from staying up too late working, feeling stressed, and falling behind further. These catch up sessions should be short but fairly frequent to make sure you keep focus and productive. Any longer than 1-2 hours will be unproductive. You should schedule catch up periods every few days in the first couple of weeks of your revision plan. They should become more frequent if you use them a lot and as you progress in your timetable – as you will revise more and more content, you will need more and more catch up periods! If you find that you don't need these catch up periods, then you should use the time to revise more topics or to relax!

WHERE YOU SHOULD REVISE

To revise, you need a comfortable and distraction free area in order to fully focus. The place you work in will partially determine how productive you are, and in turn, how stressed you feel. It is really important that you avoid revising in your bedroom or even your house, if possible. By avoiding this, you are giving yourself a physical separation between the place you work and the place you relax. If you work at home, then be strict with yourself and don't work in bed. During revision periods, some students find themselves feeling guilty for relaxing rather than working all the time. Remember that you need to relax and you should take time to unwind and reset. By having separate physical spaces where you work and relax respectively, you are training your mindset to be able to relax when you should relax (i.e. when you're going to sleep!). This is really useful for later in the exam period when your stress levels naturally increase.

> **Key Point:** Keep work and relaxation separate to help you get in the right frame of mind!

To achieve your major revision goals, choose a quiet or silent place to do your 'serious' work. This might mean working in a different place to your friends to prevent distractions. You may usually work in noisier environments, like a coffee shop, but remember that routine university work is different from revision and will probably require a different environment. You might think that working in complete silence is the best way to focus, but some students actually find low levels of background noise helps them focus, so try out both environments and see what works for you! Remember, every day is different so you might find you want to change noise levels depending on how you feel. Be flexible with your habits and yourself!

Whatever university you go to, there will be plenty of spaces to work at. Usually, there are multiple libraries, each for a different subject area with dedicated collections of books. Most universities require you to be studying a related course to access a subject library, but some universities have open access to all libraries. You may also be able to book seminar or private study rooms in your college or faculty to work in. You might like the first place you pick to study in, but if you don't feel comfortable or productive in your chosen study place, try a new one! The desk sizes, chair brand, natural light levels, and availability of fresh air if different across all the facilities offered by the university, so eventually you'll find a place you can work happily in. If you have any access needs, your university disability service will have a detailed outline of the library facilities but also will help to enable you to study, for example, if you need a special type of desk or chair to work in, they can often contact the library you would like to use to put the kit in place for you to work.

> **Key Point:** Use all the resources and assistance available to you to access facilities you need.

HOW YOU SHOULD REVISE

It is important to realise that there is no correct way to revise. In fact, there are hundreds of ways that students focus and learn their exam content. If you took exams whilst at secondary school, you may be familiar with some techniques already. Be open minded during your revision – what worked before might not be suited to university level exams. In this section, we will go over a few main revision techniques but before we go any further, ask yourself when your learning has been particularly productive – this could be during a lesson or independent study. What method were you using? Using that method or technique could be a good place to start!

Throughout this revision process, it is important that you reflect on your progress and how you feel about your progress. If you aren't remembering or understanding concepts, you might just be tired and need some time to reset. However, it might be a good idea to consider changing your revision technique or strategy. Make sure you reflect on your progress at least every 3 days. Some students like to reflect on each day's progress but that can be counterproductive because by reflecting on your progress at the end of the day, there is little time to reverse your position. Instead, students then spend the night worrying about their productivity and have a stressful time the morning after, trying to be doubly productive. As such, a good time to reflect on your progress is lunchtime or in the morning!

Make sure you keep a record of your progress so you can keep track of what you have achieved and what still needs to be learned. This can be a copy of your curriculum that you highlight once you've revised each section or you can write out a spreadsheet or word document with each topic on. Crossing things off a list can really encourage you further in your revision and reinforce your achievements. Be mindful that at the start of your revision timetable, there will be a lot of unchecked items and this might pressure you to work more and more. Once you have carefully crafted a revision plan as described above, trust your schedule and trust yourself – don't overwork at the beginning, stick to your plan and only adapt it if your progress shows you need to adapt it!

> **Key Point:** Keep some sort of master checklist of all topics you need to revise. Update this regularly (even daily!) to keep track of what you have achieved and what is still left to do.

It may be difficult to keep motivated during revision and if you find your focus waning, revisit your SMART goals for this revision period. Remember what you wanted to achieve and why. Visualise successfully opening your results and finding the grades you dream for! Your hard work will transfer into your exam performance – use your goals to re-motivate and re-energise yourself to face another day of revision!

> **Key Point:** Look back to your SMART goals – re-motivate yourself and resist revision distractions!

There are several techniques you can use to revise. Here, we have collected the main methods students use and outlined their strengths and weaknesses. These methods are generally transferable and so suit multiple exam types – and students! Each method can be used to achieve all the key foundations of good revision we have discussed in this chapter, like spaced repetition, chunking, and enable the separation of topics into high and low priority groups.

FLASHCARDS

Flashcards are a widely used technique where a student puts a question on one side of a card and an answer on the other. Flashcards are great for factual curriculum-based knowledge memorisation because you can go through your curriculum and write flashcards that directly meet what your curriculum states. This way, you know that once you learn the whole stack of flashcards, you have memorised the entire curriculum!

The best way to use flashcards is to go through a small stack a couple of times and to more frequently cycle through the cards you don't remember. Once you are familiar with the entire stack of flashcards you have, then you can go through the entire stack at a time and just repeat the ones you don't remember. There are virtual flashcard making software like Anki, which is free and automatically applies spaced repetition to your revision for you!

Pros:

Flashcards allow you to test yourself – or enlist friends or family to help you revise! They're a great way for bulk memorisation of facts and to test yourself on your knowledge. Flashcards also a great because they are easy to split into chunks to work through and you can easily see what you've achieved!

Cons:

Flashcards don't work that well for exams that don't require a lot of memorisation. They also take a lot of time to make. If you make paper flashcards, it's unlikely that you have copies for if you lose them!

REVISION LECTURES

Lots of university courses offer a revision course at the end of the taught lecture course. These courses are brilliant for consolidating your knowledge and are usually written with the exams in mind, therefore, they contain very exam-relevant content. Sometimes these lectures are recorded, which allows you to listen back to them as many times as you want.

There are also a wide range of lectures and podcasts available on streaming platforms. If they are from reputable producers, for example a museum, faculty, or national society, then these are a great add-on resource for your revision.

Pros

If the lecture is recorded, then you can listen to it (repeatedly!) whenever your schedule has time. Lots of students find recorded lectures or podcasts good to listen to whilst they are travelling. They are a completely different presentation of information compared to books or notes, and so offers a different way to absorb information.

Cons:

Some students find these lecture courses useful only when they have a strong foundation of knowledge and when they don't, these courses can be stress inducing. You must make sure that you are listening to legitimate and correct podcasts if they are not produced by your institution.

MIND MAPS

Mind maps are a great way to present information in a very visual way. You can show how ideas link together or use a mind map to develop a concept as you expand your mind map. To use a mind map effectively, start in the middle of the page and write your 'central node', which is the main topic. Then, expand the map, with the main ideas branching off of the central node. Each branch should have a few words as a title – think of them as the headings of an essay. Expand the main ideas with more branches (think of these as subheadings) and finally, the end of the branch can be your key concept or conclusion. After completing the content of your mind map, it is useful to look over the whole network of branches and see if you can identify any common ideas or connections. Adding in annotations or highlighting your writing after creating your mind map is a great way to add to your knowledge and consolidate what you know.

Pros:

They're a great way to help memorise content because you can use different colours, positions on the page, and images to prompt your memory. For example, you may be struggling to remember the year Joan of Arc was born. You could remember that you wrote this date in gold and it was at the top right corner of the page... ah! 1412!

Cons:

Mind maps are great for thinking through concepts or presenting your knowledge but they don't have any built-in revision methods in them.

NOTES

If you have a good set of notes, then you're in a great place to start your revision. Notes are a brilliant resource but you must check that they have the right and up to date information on them – there is little use learning incorrect facts!

Pros:

Working from existing course notes means that you don't have to spend time making your resource. If you use a constant structure when writing your notes, imaging where information lies on the page can be an aid memoire. You can also edit the notes, highlight them, and annotate them as you revise.

Notes are great for information that you need to understand – not just memorise. They're also good any concepts that have a storyline to them or progressive explanation, as they provide context.

Cons:

Notes are a great information resource but they don't have any built-in revision methods in them. You can cover and uncover the notes to test your knowledge, but it can be very difficult to memorise a whole page of notes, rather than the same quantity of information in another form (like flashcards!)

If you haven't made notes before revising, they are very time consuming to write out. You may also mistake writing out the notes for learning them – a lesson many students have learned the hard way!

PAST PAPERS

Past papers are one of the best resources you can use during revision. We've already outlined how you can use past papers to effectively plan your revision but you also need to use past papers to revise! Use the most recent few as mock papers. This means you don't look at the questions (except for when you were planning your revision!) until you sit down to do the mock paper in simulated exam conditions. You should plan when you are going to do these exams – it's most useful to do the first one about 2-3 weeks before your official test because you can then use it to check in with how you are performing, use it as extra motivation, and to guide any alterations to your revision strategy if needed. You should then do the remaining mock exams closer to the test as a mechanism to revise and recall information. You can decide how many mock exams you want to do to feel ready for the exam, typically 3 or 4 is ample for practise.

You should work through the rest of the past papers as you revise. The best way to use past papers is to make a directory of questions so you can revise a topic then go straight to practising writing a question on what you've just learned. Make sure you mark the papers with the official mark scheme, or if you don't have one, be strict and use your lecture notes, syllabus or a textbook to mark your exam. Marking the exam is a good exercise in itself because it makes you go through your answer with a fine-tooth comb and learn how you score more marks. You can even take notes whilst you're marking your exam paper so you have the information consolidated in one place and can look back at what you have learned.

MEMORISATION TRICKS

Acronyms

Strictly speaking, an acronym is a word that is formed from the first letters of a list of words. However, lots of students use a string of random assortments of letters as their acronyms if they find they can remember them. By having a prompt that you can easily remember, it chunks the information down into associated group and makes the information easier to retrieve, therefore, to remember! An example is: HOMES which stands for Huron, Ontario, Michigan, Erie, and Superior – the five Great Lakes in the United States.

Associations

To use associations as a memory trick, you associate new facts with things or places you already know, for example, my friend Alice lives at 27 New Street and there are 27 bones in the hand. To remember the fact, I'd ask myself where does Alice live? This technique is really handy for small factual memorisation but requires you to have an object, person or place that already exists to hook the new knowledge onto.

Diagrams

Different information can be digested more easily in a picture or diagram. Make the diagram or picture very simple whilst including all the information you need. You may also find that remembering a graph and rough shape of data points easier than remember a list of numbers.

Memory Palaces

This memory technique uses your spatial memory and associations to help you remember sequences of information. Make the information you're trying to memorise into a picture or image. Then, you choose a location you know well, perhaps your house, and then imagine your first image of information. Then, proceed to walk through your house and associate a mental image of the information in each room.

Songs

Singing things can use different memory pathways than normal memorisation and be a really effective way of remembering information. Choose a song you know and life and try to fit your information into the lyrics. This can be quite time consuming to do, but you may find that it is useful for the information that refuses to stick in your memory!

Teaching

Teaching a topic to someone can help you remember it because you need to explain concepts and truly understand them. You don't need to prepare a full presentation or paper, instead you can enlist friends and family to give mini lectures on topics. This also can help to associate information with a person, giving you another association to guide your memory!

MINDFULNESS DURING REVISION

The period during which you are preparing for exams can be emotionally turbulent. It is completely normal to feel out of control, anxious, stressed, or sad. If you are feeling emotional, the first thing you need to do is take a deep breath. Then, ask yourself if you are feeling a normal emotional reaction from your normal baseline. If this is hard to tell, ask yourself if your emotional response is proportional to the situation. If you find yourself in tears over a broken cup or stressed that making lunch takes too much time in your revision schedule, then you may be experiencing burn out or something else than just exam provoked stress. Talk to someone you trust, a healthcare provider, or a university counsellor – just talking could help you re-centre and re-focus, and if you do need some extra support, then you will be in the right place to access it.

Many students find that the pressure of exams and revision can sometimes feel overwhelming. Working and living in a state of heightened stress and emotion is not productive or healthy. To proactively prevent this overwhelming feeling, you should take regular breaks away from work. Try to spend time outside away from your computer screen and work. One effective way to make sure you have time outside to relax is to arrange with a friend (preferably one that isn't sitting the same exam as you!) to go for a walk at a certain time. Unfortunately, the weather in the UK is not always permitting for outside excursions, but you might find a more relaxing space, like a nice coffee shop to treat yourself to a hot chocolate in, or a covered area outside to sit in and relax. Other things that you can build into your approach to revision and can help manage revision related stress include setting a bedtime that you routinely follow, eating a balanced diet (with plenty of snacks!), and have some social interaction even during your most intense work periods.

> **Key Point:** Be deliberate in planning time to relax and reset – revision is a marathon not a sprint!

If you find taking a break isn't enough to make you feel significantly more centred, then your university and local health service can recommend free apps that are designed to give your mind some space. Lots of well-known apps like 'Calm' or 'Headspace' have student subscription discounts so it's worth investigating to find an app that suits you. No matter what university you go to or your level of stress, there will always be plenty of people you can talk to, including friends, your university counselling service, faculty mentors, supervisors or department advisers, and nurses or doctors.

What to do if you're having a stressful moment

1. Take a deep breath. Feel your breath go from your nose all the way to your chest. Hold your breath for a second and then slowly breath out. Be present for your breath.
2. Actively take account of your body – wiggle your toes and fingers, then move your legs and arms, lastly stretch your neck
3. Ask yourself why you are feeling stressed
4. Reflect back on what you have achieved thus far.
5. Take a break if you need some head-space
6. Set an achievable SMART goal to focus on in the next 30 minutes – I hour.

COMMON REVISION RELATED WORRIES

"I don't feel like I've done enough revision compared to my friends"

Almost every student, regardless of how much revision they got under their belt, thinks this - you are not alone! If you have started revising, it can be help to look back at your checklists and see how much you have achieved. Often this is quite reassuring! If you haven't gotten that far on your revision journey, trust the timetable and plan you have devised, take a deep breath, and carry on!

"I just can't focus"

This is a common issue whilst revising – consider doing shorter bursts of work like using the Pomodoro method discussed earlier in this section. You may want to change your study environment or the time you work. Be strict with yourself and make sure you're getting enough sleep! Lack of focus can be frustrating but it is fixable.

"I feel like I'm really struggling but no-one else seems to be finding this hard"

It's human nature to compare ourselves with others and you probably know that it isn't a productive activity already! Just like you have peaks and troughs of focus, productivity, and emotion, your friends will too. Your schedules and cycles aren't the same, so just because your friends may not be feeling overwhelmed simultaneously to you, doesn't mean that they aren't experiencing similar doubts and feelings. People all react differently to stress and some are very private with their feelings and others less so. What helps to break this worry is talking to your friends or peers and then you will get an idea of the shared experience, and feel not so alone!

"'I am not doing well when I test myself with past papers"

Having empirical evidence of your achievement can be reassuring but it can provoke further anxiety. Firstly, look at the exam, was it full of niche questions? Did the exam just ask every topic you were weak on? This is simple to fix – learn from this exam and move on. Do another past paper if this will reassure you.

If you are struggling generally with the content, depending on how close your exam is, it may be worth altering your revision strategy and timetable: re-analyse what the exam will test you on, make sure you have a firm grip

TIME MANAGEMENT

This section is dedicated to sharing time management skills and how to approach deadlines. The most important takeaway from this section is to organise your workload so that you have time to relax and take care of yourself. Work – life balance is a crucial skill to develop during your time at university. Research has shown that time to reset and relax has a positive impact on academic work, exam results, and health in general. Good time management is the foundation of having a good work-life balance.

University deadlines come in all shapes and sizes. Examples of deadlines can be a short-term goal, like an essay or question sheet to do, or could be more long-term, for example writing a dissertation. This chapter will explain how to approach work, deadlines and importantly, how to juggle multiple deadlines or assignments. These techniques can also be applied to examination preparation. By the end of this chapter, you will be introduced to several ways to manage your workload and time. You may be familiar with some approaches already or even have tried some before. It's important to be flexible with your approach to time management because things that worked 6 months ago may not be as effective as they used to be, and things that did not work for you before, might be effective now! Other approaches may work with some types of work, like essays, but not presentations. One size doesn't fit all, and you and your work load will change over time, so don't be afraid to try new strategies.

WHEN SHOULD I WORK?

Lots of students have a false expectation that productivity is directly related to starting work earlier. This might be true for some students, but for others, turning up to the library at 8am can be an unproductive and inefficient use of time, ultimately leading to more work-related stress. Don't feel pressure to work when your friends are working or when you feel you 'should' be working.

During university, you need to figure out what time you work best. To gauge where to start, you can be guided by your sleep pattern: if you are a night owl, your attention probably peaks in the afternoon and evening, and vice versa for early birds. Be aware that different tasks and work assignments can require different mindsets and levels of attention. You might find you can do work for one class really well in the morning and another in the afternoon. As such, it's important to approach your time and productivity levels with an open mind and try different things!

The after-lunch work lull is a common phenomenon to students and people in the workforce. This isn't just due to eating too much tasty lunch, but also because of how your body physically functions. Every day, each person will feel more tired and less attentive in a short period somewhere roughly between 1pm and 3pm. This is because of the hormone in your body called 'cortisol' which plays a major role in wakefulness. At around 1pm-3pm (it varies between people), the level of cortisol in your body drops, leaving you more tired and unable to concentrate as well as other times. You can take advantage of this, by scheduling non-work tasks during this time – it may be a siesta, food shopping, or time for a walk! The important take-away is that you will feel a cycle of being productive and unproductive throughout the day and you should structure your day to suit this. There is little point forcing yourself to sit at your desk and not really being productive, rather than being flexible with yourself and your schedule.

Finding the times that you are most productive is important for working towards long-term goals. However, there might be times during university where you need to crack on and work, despite how ready to work you are feeling. The pressure of a looming deadline or exam will be a big source of motivation for productivity, but only if you use it productively. The tips in this section will help you structure your time and, therefore, indirectly manage your stress to a manageable level. Using these techniques, you should be able to work during most situations and deadline pressures, but remember, optimal work and optimal productivity will come in cycles.

Key Point: Experiment with different times of working to find out what is best for you!

HOW LONG SHOULD I WORK?

There is no rule about how long you should work for before you have a break, however, it is generally said that you should have at least 10 minutes break every hour. Some students set a timer for a certain time block and let their timer dictate break time. Others prefer to work until they want to take a break. Either is a valid approach, just adjust the break time proportionally to how long you have worked for. For example, if you've worked for 2 hours without taking a break, take a 20-minute rest.

A popular student study technique is called the Pomodoro Technique and involves listing out tasks and allotting 25-minute work blocks (called a Pomodoro) to each task. Then, you work for one pomodoro and take a 5-minute break before cracking on with the next pomodoro. You can give a task one pomodoro to work in, or you can give it 5 – it's up to you. The Pomodoro technique is a good way to work if you struggle to focus for a long time because you just take it 25 minutes at a time. It's quite popular for small to medium sized work tasks, like question sheets or writing an essay section.

> **Key Point:** Take regular breaks whilst working. Decide if you're going to structure these breaks or take them as you feel like it!

HOW TO APPROACH YOUR FIRST DEADLINE:

Ok so it's happened! You have received your first piece of official work that you need to hand in to your professor. This is usually an essay or problem sheet (a list of questions to complete, usually in mathematics-based subjects like engineering or physics). Usually your score for your first assignment doesn't count towards your final module grade, or counts for a very small percentage. It's natural to be nervous, but try to see the assignment as an opportunity to see how you are doing academically and a chance to try out your strategies to approaching assignments.

1. Make sure you know the *exact* deadline that the lecturer means. If the deadline is Wednesday 10th March, this could mean different things to different lecturers! For example, it could mean by 12 noon on Wednesday 10th March or it could mean 11:59pm Tuesday 9th March.

2. Break it down into sizeable chunks. This means that the workload is less overwhelming, and you can easily tell if you're on track for your deadline! For example, your essay is entitled 'What was the most important factor contributing to world war 1?'. Chunk the whole task of writing an essay down into tasks:

   - Review relevant lecture slides and notes
   - Read recommended book chapters. Take any relevant notes. If there isn't a reading list for this particular essay, look in the lecture slides for references and citations and have a look at these resources. You can also conduct a small library search for resources (more on this in the Academic Searches section)
   - Draft out structure of essay. This also consolidates what you have read into one storyline for your essay
   - Chunk the essay into tasks: introduction, middle paragraphs each individual contributing factor, conclusion

> **Key Point:** Chunking the assignment essentially makes a structured to-do list of smaller tasks that you can then follow.

3. Write out a timetable and allocate your chunks into the time you have. It might look something like this:

Monday 1	Tuesday 2	Wednesday 3	Thursday 4	Friday 5
Review lecture slides Find library resources to use for this lecture	Read library resources	Read library resources Draft structure of essay	Look at draft structure of essay and edit if needed Chunk out essay into tasks Begin introduction	Finish introduction See how far I get with the middle of the essay

Saturday 6	Sunday 7	Monday 8	Tuesday 9	Wednesday 10
Rest day!	Read what I've written so far Finish middle of the essay	Write conclusion Proof read	Read essay Make any changes	12 noon: deadline! Submit the essay!

The timetable you make will depend on other commitments you have and you should add in any extracurricular activities or other commitments to your work schedule to block out time for them.

You might notice that this timetable does not have times to do the work by, beyond the day. This suits people who feel overly pressured with more detailed, short term deadlines. Instead, the approach to work to accomplish the list of tasks by the end of the day, giving flexibility and a broad time bracket to achieve the tasks in. Alternatively, you may want to be more specific with your time scheduling, allotting time blocks in hours or half an hour to work in. Whichever approach you choose, be realistic with your time and what you can accomplish within the time you set. It is much better to overestimate the time you will need to complete a task in, opposed to not giving yourself enough time to work in. Then, you may also adapt the timetable as you work, for example, if you are being really productive on Thursday and do everything on your timetable, you might get a head start on Friday's tasks. If you fall behind with your timetable, don't panic! More tips about managing your timetable can be found in the 'How to Revise' chapter.

Key Point: Be realistic with the time you allocate for each task.

MANAGING MULTIPLE DEADLINES

At some point during university, you will have different assignments competing for your attention. At times, this can feel overwhelming, but you just need to take it one step at a time! The best way to tackle this situation is to prioritise your tasks. Think about which work assignment is due first but also consider the difficulty of the work and how stressed you are about each assignment. You can use a matrix to prioritise your tasks, for example, the Eisenhower matrix:

	Urgent	Not Urgent
Important	Tasks that are important AND urgent. These are the tasks you need to do first!	Tasks that are important but not urgent. You need to allocate time to do these tasks after your urgent tasks
Not Important	Tasks that are urgent but not important. Is it possible to delegate these tasks to someone else?	Tasks that are not important and not urgent. You should ignore these tasks for now.

After working out what tasks are most urgent, some students choose to start the most urgent piece of work first and finish it, before moving onto the next task. This technique is most suited to urgent deadlines and students who are happy to take one item at a time on their to-do list. Other students choose to juggle a couple of tasks at a time. This technique means that students don't feel as fatigued or bored doing the same work assignment. It also prevents students from feeling stressed about only tackling one piece of work from their list of things to do.

A slightly different approach to managing multiple assignments is prioritising tasks based on the effort needed and their importance. This approach means you dedicate your time on assignments that contribute to a long-term goal. The matrix to use is the 'Action Priority Matrix':

Impact

'Quick Wins': high impact and low effort	Major projects: high impact and high effort
Other tasks: low impact and low effort	Low impact, high effort tasks

Effort

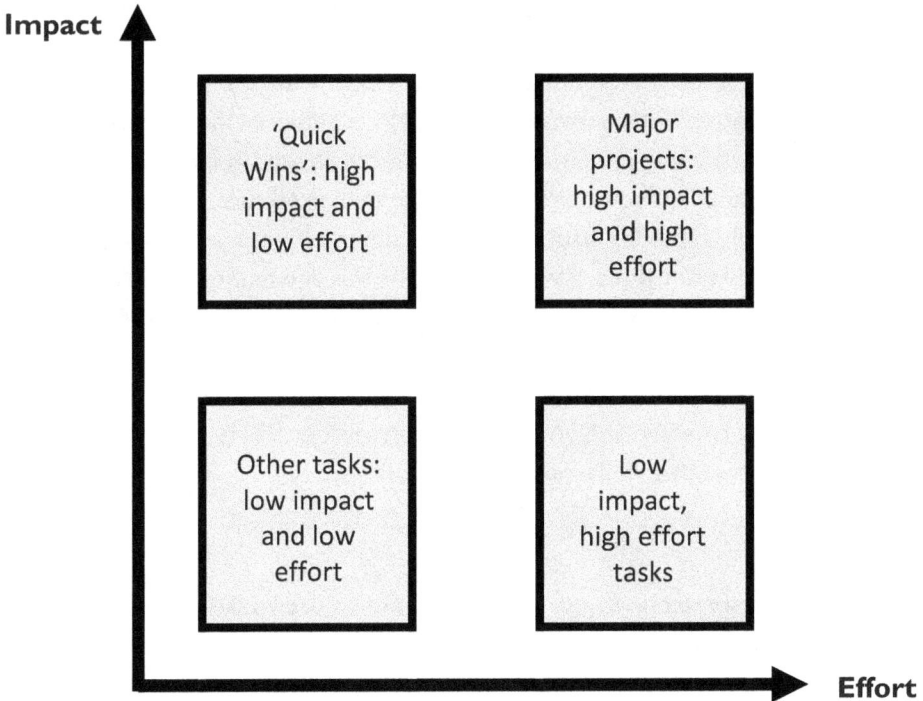

To use the Action Priority Matrix, you need to make a list of every task you have. Then give a score for each assignment for impact (0 = minimal, 10 = maximum) and effort (0 = little effort, 10 = lots of effort). Based on this, plot the tasks on the matrix. Then, do the 'quick wins' first. After completing these assignments, focus on your major projects. If you find you need a break or finish your major projects, then do or delegate your 'other tasks'. Ignore your low impact/high effort tasks until you have finished every other assignment on your list.

Key Point: Don't panic! Prioritise everything you need to do and take it one step at a time.

OVERLOADING YOUR SCHEDULE

University is full of opportunities and every student at one point finds their timetable overloaded with activities and work. It's important to recognise if you have too much going on. Signs of schedule overload can include having no 'down time' or quiet time at least once a day, feeling stressed or tired all the time, or drastically changing habits like meal times or your sleep schedule to accommodate more activities. If you are reading this and finding some elements you identify with, take a step back and consider dropping an extracurricular activity. Some students support themselves with part time work whilst studying and this can contribute to schedule overload. If this is the case, talk to your university adviser or someone your trust, and consider if it is possible to apply for a different job with a more flexible schedule.

KEY TAKEAWAY POINTS

- Pay attention to how you are feeling and adjust your work strategy to have a balance of your health and the urgency of your work
- Always break down assignments into smaller, achievable tasks to keep track of your progress and stop you from feeling overwhelmed – it's a marathon not a sprint!
- Most importantly, always be flexible in how you approach work!

HOW TO USE LIBRARIES

This chapter will give a general overview of the services and resources that your university library will offer. Your university library service will be a huge asset to your studies and this chapter will help you to take full advantage of the services offered. The university library service will hold several inductions and introductions during your Freshers' week that will teach you how to access the library, online services, and other resources. Many students find the prospect of going to a library induction during the sociable Freshers' week to be a bit of a dull prospect but ultimately find it to be an invaluable experience when their first work assignment is given!

Your university will probably have a general library, subject libraries, faculty libraries, and specific smaller collections focussing on one particular subject area. Usually, if you are a student of the university you can access every university library, regardless of your course. Oxford and Cambridge also offer college libraries within the grounds that are exclusively used by the college's student body. Linking all of these libraries will be an online system where you can look up books and resources and manage your book loans. This system is usually linked to your university account and you will be shown how to login in during your Freshers' week orientation.

Library opening times can vary between university and even between individual libraries, so check before you go! Some libraries are open 24 hours per day and 7 days per week, but others will have more restricted access. It's important to note that due to historic traditions, shops and libraries often have shortened opening hours on Sundays.

> **Key Point:** Make sure you go to a library services induction session during Freshers' week!

BOOKS

Your school or local library will have plenty of books and university libraries are the same! There will be multiple copies of popular textbooks and course related literature available, usually in stock at the subject library. The main adjustment you will have to make at a university library is navigating the vast shelves and stock they hold. If you have a particular book from your reading list you are trying to locate, you should look this book up on your library's online system. The system will then tell you how many copies are available or when they are due back, where the books are located, and if there is an option to read an online copy. You need to be mindful that there may be multiple editions of the book available and older versions may contain incorrect information.

After you have located the book online, you can reserve the book for collection in person. This means that you don't need to go to the shelf where the library keeps the book, rather a librarian will find the book for you and have it ready at the administration desk for you to collect. This service is really useful if you have multiple books to find as you can avoid spending valuable time locating each book. Please note that reservations aren't collated across libraries for you – for example, you may reserve books at different libraries but you will have to go to each library to collect the respective books rather than them being transported and available for you at one single location.

> **Key Point**: Reserving books guarantees your access to them and can save you valuable time.

You don't have to reserve books to collect them from the library, instead you can use your university online system to see where the books are shelved. University libraries will use the Dewy Decimal system to catalogue their books. This system is used universally in libraries and once you master it, allows for quick and easy access to books. All you need to find your book is the book's Dewey Decimal call number, which will be made of 3 digits, a decimal point, and 3 more digits, looking something like this:

040.148

The first 3 digits in the call number show the general book category. The Dewey Decimal system has 10 general book categories which are numbered between 000 and 999. In the example call number above, the call number shows that the book is under 'Generalities'.

Dewey Decimal Group Number	Topic
000	Generalities
100	Philosophy and Psychology
200	Religion
300	Social Sciences
400	Language
500	Natural Sciences and Mathematics
600	Technology (Applied Sciences)
700	The Arts
800	Literature and Rhetoric
900	Geography and History

The call number above tells you a more specific area within the 000 zone – the shelves will be labelled clearly so finding area 040 will be easy! After you have located the specific area the book is in, you should consult the next digit in the Dewey Decimal call number and search the area for it. Just as the library will be laid out numerically for the group number, the small areas within the group will be laid out numerically, making it easy to locate a shelf. The second and third numbers after the decimal point can help you further narrow down where your book is on the specific shelf. You don't need to memorise the above table as your library will have helpful posters around, but it's important to understand the principles of the system. Using this system for the first time can be a bit overwhelming, especially in a large library so don't hesitate to ask a librarian for some help if you need it!

Key Point: The Dewey Decimal System describes a progressively more specific book location, from left to right.

In some libraries, some books are stored 'off site' because the library has too many books to keep in the actual library. To access these, you will be able to request them through your university's online system and they will be available for collection at the library the next day. It is also important to note that some books will not be available for loan, rather you must read and use them in the library. Students can find this really annoying, especially if they don't usually work in that particular library or find the library opening hours restrictive. To solve this problem, lots of libraries have a 'scan and go' service, where you can ask for a book chapter or section to be scanned and sent to you digitally. These scans generally expire within 2 weeks but can be re-requested if you need further time. You may also be allowed to photocopy book sections yourself – this will be indicated on the front of the book cover.

This section has addressed how to access a book if you already know which book you want to borrow. You can also use the university library online system to find books by typing in a topic or an author. Lastly, if you find that your library does not have a book you need, you can request the library to buy it and add it to their collection.

Key Point: Don't buy a book if you can't find it in the library – ask the librarians to add it to the library collection!

JOURNAL ACCESS

Whatever your course is, at some point you will need to access primary research literature from academic journals. Most academic journals do not publish paper hard copies of journals and if they do, your library will probably only have one paper copy that is for reference use only. As such, you will access most, if not all, of your research articles online. Few articles are accessible free of charge when you search for them online, with most behind expensive pay-walls. Luckily, your university will have a subscription to the major publication houses and journals. To access the articles, you should scroll down on the article page and click 'login via institution'. The page will ask you to select your institution (here, you should choose your university) and then will take you into your university login page.

If your university does not have a subscription to the journal you need to access, you can request for them to subscribe but unlike requesting for new books, setting up a subscription often takes a long time to process. If you really need the article and in a short time frame, you should look at the article's authors. One author will be designated as the 'contactable author' and should have their email address published beneath the author information. You can email any author and they can send you their manuscript free of charge. Please note, the author may not reply to you and if they do, the manuscript you receive will be a pdf copy of the article that was published in the journal.

> **Key Point:** You can use your library or university account to access journals and articles for free.

DATABASES

Some libraries will have copies of databases created by the university academics or departments. These databases can be used by any student and rarely need extra permissions or access codes. The data stored is a good resource if you have a specific project and the dataset is suitable to answer your research questions, but is a useless resource if it doesn't fit your project. Generally, students use the library database copies if they already are using the database through their departments and there are temporary technical issues with the departmental access gateway. Regardless of the limited usefulness of the databases available through the library service, it's important to know that you can sometimes access them through the library service.

> **Key Point:** The university library will have some databases available for use. These can sometimes save you time as the data is already collected and ready to use!

ARCHIVES AND COLLECTIONS

Archives and collections store rare books and resources (including historical artefacts) specific to a time-frame or person. As such, it's easier to think of an archive or collection as a mini museum rather than a shelf of books. For students studying humanities or social sciences, you will come across the archives and collections when you are approaching your dissertation or research project. Unlike going to the library to find a book, you often need to contact the archive or collection to arrange a time to access the material. Sometimes you may even need to be accompanied by the collection's librarian whilst viewing the material.

You should be mindful that your work does not decide the archive or collection you will use. Instead, you and your supervisor will synthesise your research question based on the archives and collections available to you. In rare circumstances, this may even mean forming a collaboration or applying for permission to access another institute's archive. As such, knowing what archives and collections your university library holds is key to taking full advantage of the resources available to you. You can find a list on your university library website or contact the head archive librarian for more information.

Key Point: Contact the archivists early in your project to learn how you can access the material.

SEARCH SERVICES

University libraries often offer 'search support' for academic searches. At the start of an original research project or dissertation, one of the first tasks is to see the existing work and evidence relevant to your question. This is done through academic searches of public academic databases such as PubMed, Scopus, and JSTOR. Your academic search will involve looking for specific key words or phrases, potentially within a certain time frame. To complicate things further, each database will have a different way of formatting searches but it is essential that whilst you are changing the search format, the search itself stays the same. This was a very brief overview and in no way covers all that you need to know when synthesizing an academic search but hopefully it conveys the complexity of the task! The library staff often has an expert search librarian who can help you with formatting and improving your search. When the time comes for you to embark on original research, you should contact the librarian specialising in academic searches early on in your project to maximise the help they can offer!

> **Key Point:** Academic searches are really complicated but the university library often has an expect librarian who can help you! Please also see the Academic Search chapter for more information.

WORKSHOPS

Libraries often host workshops for all university students to access for free, including wellbeing workshops, academic focussed workshops, and writing classes. Wellbeing workshops often have guest speakers or counsellors in to talk through strategies to manage your mental and physical health whilst studying. Some libraries even offer dedicated meditation classes for students. To find out more information about the wellbeing initiatives run by your university library, look on the internal website or the university's wellbeing pages.

Academic workshops run by the library are a great way to learn skills that you are expected to know or develop at university but aren't necessarily taught. This can include time management skills, statistics workshops, and referencing. Another popular library run initiative is writing classes, where students attend to sit in a silent room with other students and write their essay or dissertation. These classes are great for students who need a structure or social expectation to not talk and get on with work!

> **Key Point:** Your university library will host a range of workshops and classes to support your studies – make sure you have a look at what is on offer on the library website.

WORK SPACES

Libraries also can offer a variety of spaces to work in, including silent study spaces, group work rooms, and computer rooms. We touch on work spaces in the How to Revise chapter, but due to the importance of the topic, we will go over a few more details here.

During your time at university, you will find you work better in certain environments. At the beginning of your degree, it's crucial to be flexible with your work environment and try out different work spaces, noise levels, and work schedules to find the environment that suits you best. Typically, a library will have several different types of work environment for you to choose from, with different sized desks, chairs, levels of natural light, and noise levels. It'll take you a while to try out every single library and work space so try to experience a few different environments to help narrow down those that you prefer. Please note, some libraries will require you to pre-book your seat so check before you go!

If your chosen library doesn't require you pre-book your seat, don't feel like you need to arrive at opening time to get one! Other students will have classes to attend throughout the day, so there is generally a good turnover of desk space. Be mindful during exam season, as libraries are a popular place to work with some desks occupied all day, so you may need to arrive around opening time to get a place to work.

In addition to computer access and desk space, libraries can also have other facilities and equipment to facilitate your study, such as printing, photocopying, and scanning machines. There may also be headphones available to enable you to listen to resources without disturbing other library users. If you find you need something to study, ask the library desk if they can lend you it – they're usually well equipped to help!

ACCESSIBILITY

If you are a student who needs some support to access the library or have a long-term health condition, please let your library know, usually via the Disability Advice Service (DAS). Libraries can offer a range of services to support you through your university experience. Here we will outline some of the common services available but please note, this section is not exhaustive and often libraries can offer further, personalised support if you have a specific unmet need. We hope this section can alleviate initial worries about access to libraries and empower you to access the support you need to thrive.

Most modern libraries are designed to be accessed by all students, with lifts, ramps, magnifiers and ergonomic furniture readily available. Usually, special equipment such as ergonomic furniture is only available in specific rooms or upon asking at the library front desk. You can find out more details about access, including parking facilities, through your university library website or by contacting the access and equality librarian team. Most libraries will offer a one-to-one consultation with you to make sure you can easily access the libraries and study comfortably. Please be aware, that some universities are based in very old campuses, some dating back to the 1200s. This means that sometimes physical access to some collections may be difficult for those with mobility difficulties. If this applies to your faculty library or college library, usually arrangements are made so that you can access the books you need and dedicated adapted space to study elsewhere.

If you have a visual impairment, your university library and university disability service will work together to supply materials in enlarged font or with any other adaptation you require. If you have a support worker or support animal then the university library can offer them a free reader's card so they can access the library with you when needed. You often need to contact the library admissions office to sort this out or in some university it will automatically be issued to you and your support worker.

In addition, most libraries will have a ready-made library toolkit available which can include:

- Magnifying glasses
- Coloured acetate sheets
- Coloured paper
- Ear plugs
- Book rests and book supports
- Daylight mimicking lights
- Ear plugs
- Dog water-bowl and assorted accessories to occupy your support dog whilst you work

Key Point: Your university disability advice service can help you to formulate an official learning plan to support your learning. Most libraries will be equipped with everything you need to study!

ACADEMIC SEARCHES

Academic searches are organised searches that identify relevant sources and evidence to your question. Throughout your university course, you will need to conduct searches of academic literature, either as part of your course work or thesis, or just to find useful sources. You may run academic searches as the first step of a systematic review of metanalysis. Whether these are formal searches or not, they should all follow the same steps.

STEP 1: DEFINE YOUR SEARCH

There are multiple strategies to define a search, but often these can overcomplicate what should be a straightforward step. All you need to do is identify the broad topic and your main focus:

- Broad topic: Sports participation in teenage girls
- Main focus: Self – esteem
- Topic stated as a   "In adolescent females, how effective is
  question: participation in sports in improving self-esteem?'

This three – step method is useful for a lot of general searches, but there are some specific techniques you can use for distinct topics. For example, if you are searching a medical topic, you should form your question with the PICO model:

- Population   What specific population will you focus on?
- Intervention   What will you change and how will you do so?
- Comparison   What is the comparison you will make?
- Outcome   What will you measure?

Whichever strategy you choose to use to define your strategy, you next need to identify and list any key words you will use in your search. Using the example above, you might list out:

- Adolescent females
- Sports
- Self esteem

Then you should also list out any words or key phrases that might be used instead of the words above, for example, 'sports' could also be listed as 'physical activity' and 'self – esteem' could instead be written as 'self – confidence'. You may want to include these alternate key words in your search too, to ensure you cover a wide range of relevant terms and include all the relevant resources in your search return. It is always worth asking your lecturers whether there are any specific search models that they recommend for your course.

> **Key Point**: Dedicate some time to properly define your search and select your key words – your whole search will be based off this so it's worth spending time to get it right!

STEP 2: SEARCH LOCATIONS

There are a wide range of databases online and a vast quantity of information in your university library which you could use in your search. If you are performing your search for a larger work assignment, like a dissertation or thesis, you should consider using physical data like grey literature and archives in your search. Usually for smaller searches, students use online databases that are subject or field specific. This is due to two reasons: firstly, because the searches are automatic and, therefore, quicker than searching physical information. The second reason is because the online databases often have the most recent and up – to – date research, although you should be aware that you may miss out older literature when using online databases.

> **Key Point:** You can use one or more databases in your academic searches. If you have the time, you can even hand search paper resources and archives too!

STEP 3: SEARCH STRATEGY

Because academic searches are organised and systematic searches, the process of entering your search into a database is slightly more complicated than using general search engines. Instead, you need to put in an organised and structured list of key terms that you want to search the database for. Searches can be really precise, so make sure you use the correct spelling of key words you want to include!

When you write a search strategy, you should make sure it includes the key words in your question, all of the alternative key terms (please see step 2), and truncated versions of search terms. Truncated versions of search terms search for all of the endings of a word, and is usually written with an asterisk (*). For example, a truncated term could be garden* which would search for garden, gardeners, gardens and gardener's. Using truncated versions in searches can help you include more relevant literature and save time, so you should always consider if they are applicable to your search!

Another trick is to use Boolean logic to combine search terms and key words. There are three main functions that you should be aware of:

- OR   The OR function means that your search will return literature that mentions either words or both.
- AND   AND function means that the search returns literature that mentions both key words. It will not return literature that only has one of the key words in
- NOT   NOT will exclude literature that includes this key term. This function is rarely used, as it can result in accidentally missing out relevant literature

Lastly, if you want to search for an exact phrase, use quotation marks, "like this", to search the phrase. Again, be mindful that this means that the search will be very specific and won't return results written as "like – this" or "likethis", potentially missing out relevant literature from your search results.

If you include more than one database in your search, be careful with the formatting of your search. Each database may format their searches slightly differently, so you must never copy and paste your search strategy from one database to another! If you don't check the unique formatting each database uses, then you may accidentally alter your search from one database to another.

> **Key Point:** It's vital to ensure your search strategy looks for the same literature across all of the databases you are using. This might mean you have to reformat your search between databases

STEP 4: REFINING YOUR SEARCH

Sometimes, academic searches can return thousands of literature items. If this happens, it means that your search is not specific enough and needs editing. To refine your search further, you can:

- Use Boolean terms where possible
- Restrict the publication language to English only
- Use filters in the search, for example, filter by publication type
- Restrict the publication dates in your search

In contrast, if your search only returns a few results, you should consider widening and improving it by:

- Ensuring all key words and synonyms are in your search
- Use Boolean terms where appropriate
- Consider using more key words – you should discuss this with your supervisor
- Add more databases to your search

Refining your search will change the scope of your question, so you should always discuss this with your supervisor!

> **Key Point:** If you end up with too little or too many search returns, you have to edit the scope of your search. Your supervisor is the best person to help you with this!

STEP 5: SAVING YOUR SEARCH

You should always save your searches after you have run them. You may need them for your final manuscript or thesis write up (often they are included as an appendix) or you may need to run the searches later in your thesis to catch any recently published work. It usually takes less than three clicks to save your search and this can save you hours, rewriting or remembering your search items later!

Most databases will allow you to print, save, export, or email your search. After you have selected one of these options, you are usually given the choice to save your search strategy and/or your search return items. Many students only save their search strategy so they can rerun their search, but then realise that they need to compare their new search results with the old search returns. As such, try to save as much as you can from your original search!

> **Key Point:** Always save your search because you may need to submit it as part of your manuscript!

STEP 6: WHERE TO SEEK SUPPORT OR HELP WITH YOUR SEARCH

Many students understand the process of academic searches really well but find making the decisions about including keys words or refining their search quite difficult. Academic searches often provide a foundation of evidence from which you can base your work off, and so they are crucial to get right. As such, you should always discuss your academic search with your supervisor and try to develop it together! Most students find that their academic supervisor can help with questions like:

- Should I include this search term?
- What time frame should we refine the search to and why?
- How can we expand the scope of our question to get more results but stay relevant to our research aims?

You can also find a lot of support from your university library service! Your university will have a dedicated academic search librarian who is an expert in academic searches and have advised hundreds of students. These librarians can help you with search strategy, formatting searches, and often knows little tips and tricks that might help your specific search. Most students find that the university librarians can help with problems like:

- I don't know what databases to include in my search
- Is the formatting of this search strategy correct for this specific database?
- I think that this search strategy is correct but it's not working!
- I am struggling with my search and I'm not sure what I should do next
- I don't know how to formulate my research question(s)
- I don't know how to turn my research question into a bibliography

Key Point: Your supervisor and the university library service are great sources of support – make sure you take advantage of these resources to make your search as efficient as possible!

UNDERSTANDING RESEARCH PAPERS

During your time at university you will be expected to read, understand, and use research papers in your work. Depending on your degree course, you may use parts of a trial methodology in your own original research project, use an article as a reference or proof of concept in an essay, or even use the paper's conclusion to alter your own practise or work style. Please note, we discuss how to access research articles for free in the How to Use Libraries chapter.

Research articles can be almost any length from less than 1 page to 60! Additionally, you will find that a research article rarely is published on its own, instead it is often accompanied by supplementary information and appendices. Approaching a research paper can be very stressful and overwhelming due to the length, language used, and formatting of the article itself. As such, it's crucial you are familiar with what a research paper contains and have a structure to approach a paper. In this chapter, we will discuss the different types of research articles, study design, key terminology to be familiar with, and the hierarchy of evidence in research. If you are familiar with what research articles contain, please skip to the end of the chapter where we will cover how to read and take notes from a research article.

DIFFERENT STUDY PUBLICATION TYPES

Research articles can be published in many different formats. Having a conceptual level of familiarity with the different publication formats is essential to understanding and interpreting research papers, regardless of topic or subject. Here, we will briefly outline the types of publications you will come across as an undergraduate and what sort of information they contain. This section is also useful if you are thinking about publishing your original work and are not sure what format to submit your work in.

Most commonly, trials will be published as an original research article which has been peer reviewed. This means the trial write up (hereon referred to as a manuscript) would be submitted to the journal and the journal then asks several independent and impartial experts in that field to read the paper and evaluate the trial and its results. The experts will return feedback and comments that must be addressed by the authors in order for the manuscript to be published. As such, peer review is a rigorous and long vetting procedure, but ultimately it improves the standard and quality of published trials.

In more traditional journals, research can also be published as a 'letter to the editor'. These articles are much shorter – usually limited to approximately 500 words and maximum one figure – and are not peer reviewed. Additionally, letters are not published with supplementary or appendix data. This means that the letters can be published much quicker than publishing a full trial and can be used to publish novel findings that are time sensitive, sort of functioning as an announcement to the research community. Usually, research trials that are published in letter format are later followed up by a full-length, peer reviewed manuscript to provide more detail and context to the investigation. In more modern journals, articles can be published as a 'rapid communication' in a similar manner as a 'letter to the editor'.

Lastly, original work can be published as a 'case study' or 'case report' which describes interesting phenomena, for example, the discovery of a unique artefact or medical patient presentation. Multiple related case reports may be published as a 'case series'. Case studies can be peer reviewed and can also attempt to demonstrate relationships between cause and effect, but be cautious that due to their nature, the sample size will be very small.

COMMON RESEARCH TERMINOLOGY

It is important to understand the general concepts that underpin any research paper. To help you navigate the paper, we have defined some general terms used.

Research concept	Explanation
Hypothesis	A specific and testable proposition about the possible outcome of a research study. It can outline a proposed relationship between variables or difference between the groups studied.
Research Question	The research question is based on the hypothesis not the data. A research question can answer the PICOT criteria: Population: what specific population are you focussing on? Intervention: this is for intervention studies only Comparison group: what is the control to compare with the intervention? Outcome: what will you measure? Time: when will you collect results and follow up on participants?
Study power	The study power describes the likelihood that the study result is a false negative conclusion. The larger the power, the lower the likelihood
Statistical Significance	A researcher will set a boundary for what is statistical significance. The statistical significance is the level of risk the investigator is willing to accept that the trial result is down to chance. The typical boundary for statistical significance is written as $p = 0.05$ which means the likelihood of the result being caused by chance is 5%. This means that if the investigator repeats the study 20 times, the same trial result will happen 1/20 times due to chance.

Confounding Factors	Any variable that influences the independent and dependent variable. This is the more scientific term for 'control variable'
Study Limitations	The investigator should always outline any weaknesses to the study design. The weaknesses outlined does not mean that the trial result is invalid, rather are considerations if you apply the study to your trial population

In addition to these new concepts, research papers can be a minefield of technical terms and subject specific language, depending on the research area. At the beginning of your research career, it is very normal to take a long time to decipher what exactly the article is saying. Most students find highlighting unknown words and annotating them with a definition or explanation is the best way to approach unknown terms and learn from the article. Some students add this new vocabulary to a main 'cheat sheet' of new words and techniques to refer to whilst reading. It can feel like a sharp learning curve, but don't worry - as you read more papers in the field, you will begin to get more comfortable with the typical language used! Some university courses will require you to read research papers from all different specialities or eras, and it can be frustrating to constantly have to assimilate your vocabulary and knowledge to a new style of language but don't worry, you will get better and faster at adapting!

> **Key Point:** Although the language used in research papers will differ depending on subject, there are several universal research terms that you should be familiar with.

DIFFERENT STUDY DESIGN

Being aware of the different publication types that journals offer is important, but it's also important to appreciate different types of study design. Study design refers to how the study investigates the research question. Most broadly, research studies can be either descriptive or analytic. Descriptive studies compare and classify data whereas analytical research attempts to quantify a relationship between the intervention or exposure and the outcome of the study. As such, you should not extract any relationship between factors and results in descriptive studies. Both descriptive and analytical studies can be further broken down into specific study structures, described below. Often, articles will not explain the details of a study design, rather just provide the design name, so it is very useful to know the different types of study out there!

	Study Type	Description	Example
Analytical Experimental	Randomised parallel group	Each trial participant receives the intervention or control treatment, assigned randomly	Investigating the effect of chocolate compared to standard treatment on patient recovery time from the flu
	Randomised crossover	One half of the trial population will receive the trial intervention under investigation first and then the control intervention. The other half of the trial population will receive the control intervention first and then the trial intervention under investigation.	Investigating the effect of diet education classes and group exercise classes on a population's weight and physical health

	Study Type	Description	Example
Analytical Observational	Cohort study	A longitudinal study following a group of participants over a period of time. Usually, the study cohort all have a common characteristic, such as exposure to a chemical or sharing the same birth year	Investigating the effect of sex-education group of teenagers living on West Street (number of children, age of children etc0
	Cross sectional	Investigators gather data from a defined group of individuals at a set point in time. The group studied is chosen based on an inclusion/exclusion criterion set by the researchers. The investigators then measure the association between an exposure factor and outcome.	Evaluating the association between chocolate consumption and teenage acne incidence in a Manchester secondary school class.
	Case-control study	Compares a group of people with an outcome of interest with a second group of people without the outcome of interest. Each participant in the first group is matched carefully in the second group with someone very similar to them. The investigators then look retrospectively to identify common exposures	Investigating a group of people with a rare disease to see any common risk factors to developing the disease

	Study Type	Description	Example
Descriptive	Cross sectional	Identifies a defined study population at a specific point in time. Measures a range of variables but has no control of the exposure of the population to measured variables.	Recording how much chocolate a class of first year university students have eaten in the last 7 days
	Ecological or correlational	Studies the association between exposure and outcome at a population level.	Investigating the relationship between the amount of chocolate consumed per household and the number of Nobel Prizes won per country
	Case report or series	Describes unique or rare cases of academic interest	A report of a rare disease being detected in a patient at St George's Hospital, London
Other	Systematic review	Synthesises all research published on a particular question or topic	A systematic review of arts interventions in mental health
	Meta-analysis	Combines the data from individual studies using statistical methods, deriving a conclusion	A meta-analysis of evidence of honey vs lozenges to treat sore throats

Key Point: Lots of students confuse study design with study publication type – they're two different things!

LEVELS OF EVIDENCE

Every study design has innate strengths and weaknesses, regardless of what the study is investigating. Some study designs are inherently more controlled for cofounding factors and bias, as such, different study designs can offer a different strength of information. It is useful to appreciate the hierarchy of evidence when reading a research paper because you can appreciate the strength of conclusions provided (based on study design) and begin to critically appraise the paper.

In scientific research, there is a large emphasis on reducing bias, but in other subject areas bias can be acceptable, and even useful, if you can place the study in wider social and environmental context. As such, although it is important to be aware of the levels of evidence, these levels are not the ultimate defining factor of a journal article.

On the next page is a diagram that illustrates the hierarchy of evidence. As you go further up the pyramid, the research type decreases in bias and increases in ability to show causal relationships. Therefore, at the bottom of the pyramid, the evidence is the most biased and least able to demonstrate a causal relationship:

LEVELS OF EVIDENCE

Low levels of bias

Meta-Analysis

Systematic Reviews

Randomised Control Trials

Cohort Studies

Case Reports and Case Controlled Studies

Expert Opinions

High levels of bias

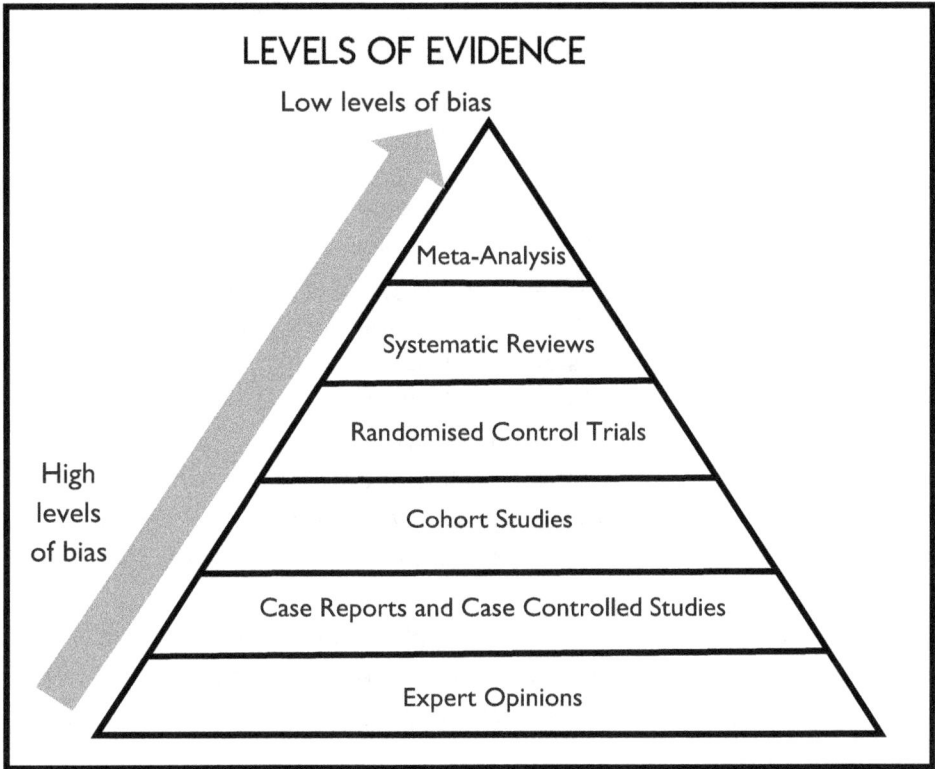

WHAT A RESEARCH PAPER CONTAINS

Regardless of study design or publication type, papers are typically organised into a standard set of sections:

- Abstract: This section is about a paragraph long and will contain a condensed version of the entire paper.

- Introduction or Background: Here, the author will present information to provide context to the study. Specifically, there will be a description about the 'problem' that the trial's question aims to address and a justification of its importance. Usually the authors will present the hypothesis and other study aims in this section.

- Methods: This section is basically a recipe for the trial. It will tell you exactly what the authors did. For larger trials and medical trials, the methods are usually brief but expanded upon in the supplementary information.

- Results: This section provides the results of the trial with no elaboration. There is usually lots of data presented in this section, alongside figures and images

- Discussion: Here, the author will discuss the meaning of the results, the wider context, and acknowledge limitations of the trial

- Conclusion: The author will address the hypothesis, investigation aims, and summarise the main findings.

- Supplementary   Information supplied extra to the central study manuscript. This information is provided to resolve a deficiency within the manuscript.

- Appendix   Information supplied extra to the central study manuscript. This information is not essential to the manuscript's completeness.

HOW TO READ A PAPER

Traditionally, university students are advised to read the paper out of order, starting with the last paragraph of the introduction to find the research question and/or hypothesis, then move on to the results and then finally the discussion. Questions that arose from reading the discussion could then be answered by reading the paper's methodology section. Although this approach is the most common strategy used by university professors themselves, it can require a degree of research experience and background knowledge to be effective, without becoming disorientated and confused.

Whilst you're becoming more familiar with research papers, we recommend you first read the abstract to get an overview of the paper. You can refer back to the abstract as you read through the paper to remind yourself of the key findings of the paper. This can help you understand why the investigators carried out elements of an experiment or emphasise certain results. For more information about how to read an abstract, please see the Understanding and Using Abstracts chapter.

We recommend you read the paper as it is written, without jumping from section to section. You can choose to skip out the methods section and refer to it only if necessary during the discussion. The methods section is important, especially if you are going to carry out similar research or experiments, but it can also disrupt the story and understanding you have gained from the introduction. We advise you to read through the manuscript's introduction, even if you are familiar with the area studied. This is because the investigator will use the introduction to describe and justify their research in the context of the existing evidence.

HOW TO TAKE NOTES FROM A PAPER

During your course, you may have to read academic articles to include in essays or other work assignments. When there is just one paper you need to read and use, it can be easy to keep track of the details and the project story, However, if you need to have a bank of papers ready to use for exams, or even just use a few in a piece of coursework, it can be time consuming and difficult to remember them correct if you haven't condensed the paper down into a good overview. Here, we will outline a tried and tested method for you to take notes from a paper!

Write the title of the paper here (or a shortened version!

First Author Surname, (Year of Publication)

Main findings:

- Write the main findings here in bullet point form
- You also should include a reason why this finding is important

Methods used:

- Briefly outline the methods used to discover this finding
- Make sure you also outline a couple of strengths and limitations about these methods so you can comment on the strength of their evidence
- This can take some research and time to do, but is worth having for revision time!

Interpretation:

- Here, you can include a brief note on the discussion points raised.
- You may also find some interesting information in the introduction to include, for example, any rationale that the study is based on

You can see that the note card you can make is brief, but contains the key information you will need for any exam, essay, or oral exam. You can adapt this note above to suit your exam or what your professors want you to include in an essay, but keep the note layout similar each time. Structuring your notes in the same way each time will act as a memory prompt if you forget any of the information!

Key Point: Taking notes from a research paper isn't just copying the abstract. Instead, you need to apply reasoning and context to the investigator's choice of experiments.

UNDERSTANDING AND USING ABSTRACTS

Abstracts are condensed summaries of journal articles or unpublished research projects seen at conferences or talks. If you want to present your work at a conference, you will often have to submit an abstract that will be used to decide who can give oral presentations and who present a poster. As such, writing a good abstract can be a very important element to create at the end of your research project. This chapter will cover how to write an abstract, and how to use abstracts effectively when you're tackling a work assignment.

HOW TO APPROACH WRITING AN ABSTRACT

Abstracts are designed to provide a brief but extensive snapshot of the entire project, including project justification and results. As such, writing a good abstract can be very time consuming and requires you to have a good understanding of your entire project. Most researchers and students will write their abstracts after completing the entire manuscript for their publication as that allows them to know the important elements of their research story they need to highlight in the abstract.

Abstracts usually follow a strict format and structure, that varies only slightly between different journals and conferences. Before you write your abstract, make sure you know the word limits and structure your journal or conference requires – it is very difficult to reformat an abstract after you have written it, because they are so structured, so it's key to write it to the brief the first time!

When you're writing an abstract, you should remember three things:

1. Make sure you use short and clear sentences, which may feel a bit artificial or abrupt compared to your natural writing style! A long and lyrical sentence can become unclear or difficult to follow, so be strict with yourself and be succinct!

2. You should define any abbreviations both in the abstract and in the text! For example,

    - British Broadcasting Corporation (BBC)
    - Magnetic Resonance Imaging (MRI)

    If you are really struggling with the word count, you can remove these abbreviation definitions, but best practice is to include these definitions.

3. You should not include citations in your abstract because it should be a self-contained summary of your original work. There is one exception to this rule – you should include a citation if your manuscript solely focuses on another piece of work, either as a rebuttal or in support. This is really rare, so in general assume that you will never create a citation within your abstract.

> **Key Point:** Abstracts function as stand-alone summaries of research. They can be required for conference presentation submissions and for article publication.

HOW TO WRITE AN ABSTRACT

The first sentence of your abstract should be factually based and introduce the general 'problem' that your research focuses on. Keep this sentence broad to provide the reader with an idea about what field you're focussing on and the wider context of the project. Examples can include:

- 7.5 million people die due to hypertension related complications
- Women's fashion reflects the gender status and role in society at the time.
- It is known that avocado plants contribute to global warming, predominantly through deforestation.

These sentences are specific to the field but don't immediately delve into the specific problem the project is addressing (unless your project is really, really broad). It's important to note that you shouldn't include a citation even with the first sentence, so make sure it's worded in your own words.

This first sentence sets the scene for the second sentence which will introduce the specific element of the problem that your research is investigating or addressing. Example sentences include:

- 7.5 million people die due to hypertension related complications. Hypertension is a preventable condition that can be modified by diet and exercise.
- Women's fashion reflects the gender status and role in society at the time. Trousers have frequently been used in society and literature to denote power.
- It is known that avocado plants contribute to global warming, predominantly through deforestation. There are several alternative methods of farming avocadoes, for example, using hydroponics.

You may use a third sentence to introduce a second specific element of your project if there are any assumptions that need to be set up and established to strengthen your project story and make the story make sense. This third sentence can also be used to narrow the scope of your project:

- Women's fashion reflects the gender status and role in society at the time. Trousers have frequently been used in society and literature to denote power. In 2021, Henley Royal Regatta (HRR) rules allowed women to wear trousers for the first time in the competition's 182 – year history.

After you have established all of the assumptions you need to set up your project story, you should introduce your project and its methods. Include your primary outcome and any secondary outcomes, if you have room. With each abstract you read and write, you will gain a small bank of your preferred ways to introduce your original project work in an abstract (and even during presentations!) Examples may include:

- 7.5 million people die due to hypertension related complications. Hypertension is a preventable condition that can be modified by diet and exercise. We randomly assigned 140 patients taking amlodipine for hypertension to either lifestyle intervention (2 hours per week of walking) or diet modification (no added salt) groups. Patients were instructed to follow their assigned regime for 3 months and blood pressure was measured every 2 weeks by the investigators. The primary outcome was the difference between the two groups in change from baseline systolic blood pressure.

- It is known that avocado plants contribute to global warming, predominantly through deforestation. There are several alternative methods of farming avocadoes, for example, using hydroponics. Here, we model the impact of changing avocado deforestation farming methods to hydroponic led strategies. Primary outcome was a change in CO_2 emission per avocado fruit produced. Secondary outcomes include financial cost and weight of avocado fruit produced.

After you have presented your project methods and measurable outcomes, you need to present your results. Just like in a manuscript, don't elaborate or explain your results, just write them factually and leave them as that! Make sure you remember to include any p values or confidence intervals, the latter in square brackets. If you have used participants in your study, it is important to include information about participation numbers (crucially, if people dropped out during the project). Once you have stated your main results, your last section will be your conclusions. This usually is about 3 sentences long, and summarises your main results in the wider context of the study and field. Try to answer your original research question or outcomes:

- Blood pressure study: There was no significant changes in blood pressure from baseline between lifestyle and diet modification groups.

- Avocado study: Hydroponic faming significantly decreased CO_2 emitted per avocado fruit. Current deforestation farming techniques cost 30p per avocado versus the modelled hydroponic cost of 45p per avocado. This cost is modelled to reduce to 20p after 3 years of farming. Lastly, there was no significant change of weight of avocado fruit produced: 20g [15 − 60]); $p > 0.05$.

As with all your academic work, make sure you get feedback from colleagues in your research group, your supervisors, and peers. However, it should be noted that abstracts written for conference submissions can have quite short deadlines, so you may need to get your supervisor to sign off on it and submit the abstract as you have written it. Students are taught to take care in their academic work throughout school and university, so it can be quite unnerving to write up your work quickly and send it off for a competition! Remember, if you're up against a tight deadline, try to be content with your best effort at the time – this is a skill that you will learn throughout your academic research career!

> **Key Point:** Try to address every important landmark in your project story within your abstract, including the context, justification for your project, outcomes, methods, and results.

USING ABSTRACTS EFFECTIVELY

Because abstracts function as a standalone summary of research, they can be very useful to use when planning work or learning about a new field of research. Please read the above 'How to Write an Abstract' section first, even if you don't need to write an abstract, to get a clear idea of abstract structures and formats. Abstracts are really useful summaries, and you should particularly use them when:

- You read a journal article
- You need to read a lot of journal articles in a short amount of time
- You need to sort articles into categories
- You need to screen journal articles for inclusion or exclusion for a literature review, meta-analysis, or systematic review.

Some professors actively encourage students to avoid using abstracts when reading journal articles because they want their students to be able to read an entire journal article and get the research story through the article independently, rather than supported by the abstract. It's up to you to decide if you are going to use an abstract to support your understanding of the article. It can depend on your priorities at the time – if you have plenty of time, you might choose to tackle an article without the abstract, or you may urgently need to write an essay, in which case using abstracts can be really helpful! The important thing is to decide your priorities and choose a strategy to suit you.

If you decide to use an abstract to help you read papers faster, first, read the abstract and identify the study aims and outcomes. Many students find it useful to take a note of the aims, with the study author and publication year. Other students find it useful to print out the abstract, highlight the main research question and annotate the abstract as they read the paper. If you are unfamiliar with the research area or have a little more time, you may choose to read the introduction to gain some context around the research question. After you have identified the research aims from the abstract, you should go to the methods section of the paper and note what methods the investigators used to answer their research question. You could annotate your abstract with the title of the experiment method or a brief explanation. Next, highlight the main result of the paper, usually declared near the end of the abstract. You should also find any other key results within the body of the article. After this, read the discussion and note down any salient points then explain or interpret the key results. At the end of this process, you should have a short set of notes and a good understanding of the study aims, methods, results and result interpretation.

Key Point: Abstracts can help you read papers faster without compromising your understanding of the research.

You may choose to use an abstract to support your understanding of a paper even if you're not on a time limit! Many students refer back to abstracts and re-read the paragraph as they read a paper. This can help remind them of the paper's aims and main results, orientating them within the large body of text. This technique is often used by students with learning differences or those who struggle with larger pieces of text. In this way, abstracts are a prompt and a guide for understanding, as they clearly describe the direction of the study.

> **Key Point:** Refer back to abstracts when reading through journal articles to re-orientate your perspective and improve your understanding of the text.

If you are using abstracts to screen papers for a research investigation, your study protocol will have clear instructions on what you should do, broken down into steps like a recipe. During abstract screening, you will read the abstract and see if the study described meets certain criteria (set out in the protocol). These criteria could be the presence of a certain key word, involvement of a population (for example, women in a certain age bracket), or the use of a specific study intervention. Sometimes it is not possible to get this information from an abstract, and your study protocol might then instruct you to read the article to decide whether to include it in your final analysis.

> **Key Point:** Abstracts can be used in research studies, for example literature reviews, to filter out less relevant studies from analysis.

AVOIDING PLAGIARISM

Plagiarism is when a student claims someone else's work as their own. This can be through:

- Copying an entire essay or section of an essay
- Copying a figure or image
- Copying a presentation
- Copying someone's interpretation of a book, quote, or other source – this can be their published idea or just their thought!

Plagiarism is one of the most serious academic misdemeanours that a student may commit. Once a student is found to have plagiarised their work, they can be expelled from the course and potentially banned from applying a course at the same institution. If you plagiarise at university and it goes unnoticed, don't celebrate yet – there have been many cases of work from decades ago being re-examined and declared to be plagiarism, ruining careers and reputations.

Plagiarism is taken very seriously, because as an academic, your work relies upon your honesty and reputation to be accepted by the research community. Once you betray this trust, it is very hard to get back.

You will be tempted to commit plagiarism at some point during your degree – maybe you're up against a tight deadline, or just don't understand the essay question. It is always better to go to your tutor and ask about the work than plagiarising. It is always better to hand nothing in (or a page of your notes or essay plan) than hand in a piece of work that you have plagiarised. Many universities use an online plagiarism checker to ensure students' work is their own. If you are ever tempted to plagiarise, ask yourself this – can you outsmart a computer?

Key Point: Plagiarism is very serious and can have devastating effects on your career.

HOW TO AVOID PLAGIARISING

So now you know what plagiarism is, how do you avoid doing it? At all levels of academia, you will be using other people's interpretations or evidence to make arguments or justifications within your own pieces of work. As such, it might seem difficult (or impossible!) to avoid plagiarising.

To avoid committing plagiarism, there are several crucial skills you need to implement whilst creating your work:

- Keep a record of the sources you consult in your research
- Paraphrase or quote from your sources
- Give the original author credit for their work by a citation and reference

> **Key Point:** You can avoid plagiarism by crediting where you have found information and ideas.

RECORDING YOUR SOURCES

Most students commit plagiarism accidentally and despite their good intentions, it is still a very serious offence. Accidental plagiarism is often committed by students forgetting where an idea came from and accidentally claiming it as their own idea. This is the easiest way you can commit plagiarism but also the easiest mistake to solve! Whilst you plan your work assignment and even as you write it, you should keep your notes organised and label any ideas you have read elsewhere with the author and source. You can even cite your notes to ensure you have an accurate record of where you have sourced ideas from. Detailed guidance on how to create citations and references can be found in The Fundamentals of Referencing chapter, but here we will outline three different versions of notes to give you a better idea of how your notes should (and shouldn't!) look like!

Note style 1:

The Christmas tree was associated with Christmas celebrations in Germany, associated with Saint Boniface. The tradition was brought to the UK by Queen Charlotte but was popularised by Queen Victoria

This set of notes has no sources acknowledged and is the typical note style that lead students to accidentally committing plagiarism. You may have found at school that it is quick to copy down information from a website or book and then move on to the next thing you need to do, but at university, the expected acceptable standard is different. You must learn to take notes properly and credit the sources you use. It will take more time initially, but will become second nature to you!

Note style 2:

The Christmas tree was associated with Christmas celebrations in Germany, associated with Saint Boniface (website www.historyofthechristmastreeatwindsor). The tradition was brought to the UK by Queen Charlotte but was popularised by Queen Victoria (page 16 of English Custom and Usage by Christin Hole (1950)

Note style 2 is a good way to quickly acknowledge sources and has enough detail to allow you to go back to the source material if you need. This method of sourcing is informal and you will have to create formal citations when you're writing up your work.

Note style 3

The Christmas tree was associated with Christmas celebrations in Germany, associated with Saint Boniface. The tradition was brought to the UK by Queen Charlotte but was popularised by Queen Victoria[2]

1. The History of the Christmas Tree at Windsor. http://www.thamesweb.co.uk/christmas_tree.htm. Retrieved 1st January 2022

2. Hole, C. English Custom and Usage. (B. T. Batsford Ltd.,1950)

Note style 3 shows the same information as before, recorded with citations and a reference list. Putting citations in your notes can save you time when writing up, but can feel like a lot of work whilst you're researching for your work assignment.

> **Key Point:** If you start with bad quality notes you may end up with bad quality work – carefully source your information so you don't accidentally plagiarise!

PARAPHRASING AND QUOTATIONS

If you want to include information into your work assignment from a source or another thinker, you can either paraphrase it or insert the information as quotation. Paraphrasing means retelling information in your own words, whereas quotations are direct reproductions of the material. Traditionally, it is thought that paraphrasing in academic writing is much better than quoting, as it demonstrates that you understand the content enough to write it in your own words. However, in reality, it is your choice to either paraphrase or quote is dependent on what you feel is right within your body of text and the information you're including. Typically, paraphrasing is most suited to describe ideas or concepts from other sources, whereas quotations can be used for things people have written or said. Usually, a paraphrased concept or idea is accompanied by an in-narrative citation (see below). An example of paraphrasing is:

Original Version:

Her life spanned years of radical changes in technology

Paraphrased Version:

Jane lived through a period of technological innovation (Smith, 2022)

To demonstrate to the reader that the information or idea in your work assignment is from another person, you can use a quotation. To make sure you avoid plagiarism, when you quote a source you should make sure that:

- You used quotation marks or format as a block quote
- The original author or thinker is correctly credited with a citation. To learn how to create a citation, please see the chapter entitled The Fundamentals of Referencing.
- The text you include is true to the original. If any changes are made, you have used correct symbols to show your editing

> **Key Point:** Quotes are a key way to clearly credit another author's work within your work.

Typically, you will use quotation marks to indicate content that is a quote, however, if you include a longer quote (approximately more than 6 sentences long), you can use a block quotation format to indicate that they are a quotation, like this:

> A block quotation begins on its own line. You should indent your block quotation, to indicate that they are not part of the main text. As you can see with this example, block quotations aren't encased by quotation marks. Sometimes, it can be difficult to judge whether to include a quotation within your essay text or as a block quotation. Some people advise that you should block quote any quotation longer than 100 words, but it is a personal decision. Formatting a longer quote as a block quote can help to organise your essay, despite being shorter than 100 words or 6 sentences.

Although a quote should be an accurate representation of the information or idea, you may need to take out a few words or insert a new word. This often happens if you are trying to embed a quote into your sentence and the syntax isn't correct. You need to format this correctly to indicate that you've edited the quote. If you have taken words out from within a quote, you can insert an ellipsis (…) where you have removed the words. An ellipsis is not needed if you remove words from the beginning or end of a quote. Sometimes, you may quote large pieces of text, and remove words from the beginning or end of the sentence within the quote. If this happens, you should use an ellipsis but also include a full stop. Four dots in a row can look odd when you read back on your work, but it is grammatically correct.

If you have added words to your quotation, you should put these words in square brackets:

> In the first line of *Moby-Dick,* the narrator tells the reader to "call [him] Ishmael."

> **Key Point:** You can alter quotations slightly to make them fit within your work better, but make sure you accurately indicate this, using square brackets or ellipsis as necessary!

GRAMMATICALLY INTRODUCING YOUR QUOTATION

Beyond including the three important things listed above, you also need to think about how to grammatically introduce a quote. This can be with commas or colons, depending on the sentence structure. If the phrase introducing the quote is not a complete sentence, you should use a comma before starting the quote:

> Quote Example 1:
>
> At the end of the book, the narrator says, "Good bye."

If the quote is introduced by what could be a full sentence (an independent clause), then you should use a colon instead:

Quote Example 2:

This is how the book ends: "Good bye."

Lastly, if the quote fits within the sentence and can be read fluently, no comma or colon needs to be used!

Quote Example 3:

In the last line of the book, the narrator tells the reader "good bye."

Key Point: It is important to introduce your quotation with correct grammar!

You may have noticed that in quote examples 1 and 2, there are capital letters but in quote example 3 there are none. If the quotation fits into the sentence syntactically, then you don't need to start it with a capital letter. However, with quotes that are introduced by a comma or colon, you should always start the quote with a capital letter.

CITATIONS

Once you have formatted your quotation, the next step is to insert a citation. As citation format can change depending on the citation style used, you should find out what citation style is most used in your area of research before writing out your citations!

The American Psychological Association (APA) style is commonly used across social sciences. With APA, you should include the author's surname, year of publishing, and the page number (if applicable). This information should be separated by commas. This structured citation can be inserted into your text in two ways, in-text or narrative:

In text Citation:

Tigers are very hungry cats, shown by "he took all the sandwiches on the plate and swallowed them in one big mouthful" (Kerr, 1968, p. 10).

Narrative Citation:

Tigers are very hunger cats. Kerr (1968) described a hunger tiger who "took all the sandwiches on the plate and swallowed them in one big mouthful" (p. 10).

Humanities subjects tend to favour using a notes and bibliography system. To cite in this style, a superscript number marks the quotation, and the citation is placed in a footnote (at the bottom of the page), also numbered with the corresponding number. This style enables you to write more information beyond the citation, for example, any notes you have about the source or further elaboration. Sometimes, the number of citations you have on a page makes the footnote half the page! Don't worry, although this looks odd when you first come across it, it is completely normal!

Notes and Bibliography System:

Tigers are very hungry cats, shown by "he took all the sandwiches on the plate and swallowed them in one big mouthful". [1]

---

1. Kerr, *The Tiger Who Came for Tea*, 10.

With this system and all the citation style examples above, you also need to include a list of all the sources you have cited at the end of the paper. Some citation styles require you to list the sources you have used in alphabetical order or the order that they appear in your work assignment. A complete guide for making a reference or citation list can be found in The Fundamentals of Referencing chapter.

> **Key Point:** You must include a citation to credit any ideas or concepts you include in your work that you have found in other sources.

THE FUNDAMENTALS OF REFERENCING

This chapter builds on the foundations of citations and referencing covered in the Avoiding Plagiarism chapter, so make sure you have read that chapter before starting on this one! In academic writing, you must credit sources of information and this can be a daunting and time-consuming process for students who do not understand the principles. This chapter will provide you with an extensive guide that will enable you to correctly tackle crediting any type of source.

WHAT ARE CITATIONS AND REFERENCES?

Citations are in-text acknowledgements of any ideas or quotes that originate from external sources. Depending on the citation style, a citation may be a superscript number or information within the text, like the author and date of publication.

If you have included a citation, you must include a reference list. This list provides more detail about the citation, enabling the reader to fully identify the source. Some students confuse reference lists with bibliographies and it's important to appreciate that the two are different types of lists – in some works, you may even have a bibliography and a reference list! A bibliography is a list of all sources you have consulted whilst writing your assignment, but aren't directly included in the work, for example, a resource should be listed in your bibliography if it helped your understanding of the topic but didn't directly influence your ideas or opinions. In contrast, your reference list contains all sources that are directly included and cited in your work. If you have both a bibliography and a reference list in your work, you should put the bibliography after the reference list.

> **Key Point:** If you include a citation, you must also include a reference list.

REFERENCING SOFTWARE

There are plenty of websites and apps that claim to be able to auto-generate references. Lots of students use these sites but find that the references generated can have advertising links embedded in them or are actually incorrectly formatted. Some apps are credible but can be prone to bugs, technical issues, and malfunction, so bear this in mind if you're writing an essay under time pressure! Your university library may have a subscription to apps with pay walls, so make sure you enquire about a university access login when you visit the library, as subscriptions can be expensive. Apps and sites like EndNote and Mendeley are generally reliable, but will often require you to manually edit some citations. As such, even if you use an automatic reference generator to write your references, you need to be able to proof read your references and correct them if necessary. This chapter will empower you with the knowledge to judge if a reference generator is creating a reference that is up to standard and guide you through how to write and edit references.

> **Key Point:** Referencing software can save you a lot of time but can be unreliable. You need to know how to correctly edit your references as necessary.

WHY YOU MUST CITE AND REFERENCE

The main reason to create citations and references is to avoid plagiarism, however, there are many other benefits, including:

- Citations and references provide evidence for your arguments, helping to validate them
- The reader has all of the information to read further into the topic, using your citations and references
- Citations and references demonstrate to your tutors and professors that you have read around the subject
- By including the sources that you have used, you demonstrate how recently published the data and information you are using. This can add context to your arguments, especially if your work is published.

- Some university assignments will mark you for your references and quality of citations. As such, it's important to get them formatted right!

> **Key Point:** The most important reason to cite and reference is to avoid plagiarism.

WHEN YOU SHOULD INSERT A CITATION

As outlined before, citations and references are key to avoiding plagiarism. Most times, it is fairly clear when you need to insert a citation – for example, when you have looked up a quotation and know that it has come from another source. However, students tend to struggle to identify when they should insert a citation when they have written content from their own knowledge base and, therefore, in their own words. Remember, even paraphrased information should be cited. As such, you should almost always cite any information or facts that you include in your essay. The only situation where you don't need to add a citation is if the information is common knowledge – for example, trees are often brown and green. This fact doesn't need citing, but if you had a piece of information that is fairly common knowledge, especially in the area that you are studying, it can be difficult to judge if something is common knowledge. If you find yourself questioning if should put in a citation, the best thing to do is to put it in. It is a serious offence to not credit an external source, whereas an occasional extra thorough citation isn't a problem.

> **Key Point:** Never write a fact down without including a citation unless it's very common knowledge.

REFERENCING STYLES

There are over 100 styles to reference with, each with different ways to format the citation and references. The styles most often used in UK universities is Harvard, American Psychological Association (APA), Nature, and the Notes and Bibliography system. Before you start your work assignment, it is crucial to find out which style your course (or individual lecturer) uses. Re-doing all of your citations in a different format is a very frustrating process, so make sure you plan correctly and save yourself from this task!

HOW TO APPROACH REFERENCING

The task of writing a completely cited and referenced essay can be daunting. As a result, some students choose to write their essay first and then go back through to insert citations, whereas others cite as they write. Although personal preference should be considered, the most important factor that should influence your decision of how and when to cite should be your notes. If your notes clearly detail where information and quotations have been sourced from (see Avoiding Plagiarism chapter), you can either cite as you write or do all your citations at the end. However, if your notes are less detailed (like the example note 1 in the Avoiding Plagiarism chapter), then you must cite as you write. If your notes aren't full of source credit details, then it is very easy to commit plagiarism as you will forget where you found different facts.

Assuming your notes are thorough and you can choose which strategy to use when referencing, you should be aware that there are benefits and drawbacks to both strategies. The cite as you write method is great because once you have finished your essay, you don't need to go back and do more work! However, students find that the fluency of their essay writing is disrupted by continually stopping to insert citations and references. If you choose the method of inserting your citations after writing your assignment, beware that almost all students feel very fed up with focussing on the same piece of work after they have finished writing the content. You need to make sure you are still diligent and focussed whilst inserting your citations.

Regardless of the method you use, after you finish adding citations and references, you need to read through your work assignment and make sure you have put citations in every place that there should be a citation. This step is often missed out by students, but it is the crucial check to ensure you produce a good standard essay that cannot be accused of plagiarism. As you go through each sentence, ask yourself

- Does this sentence contain a fact, opinion, or non-original idea?
- Does this sentence contain an original idea that relies on a fact or other existing evidence?
- Did I find this fact or opinion from a source during my essay planning?
- Did I take this fact or idea from my existing knowledge? Where did this knowledge come from?

If you can answer 'yes' to any of the above questions, you need to add a citation!

Once you have completely cited your sources within your work, the last step is to write and/or check your reference list. With some work assignments, marks can be deducted for incorrect references so checking them through is a crucial last step. When you're checking your references, the first thing to do is to make sure they are referring to the correct source. Once you're confident you're crediting the right source for the information, then you should check the reference systematically for two things:

- Is the information within the reference correct, for example, author name (including spelling), date of publication, and page numbers referenced? Sometimes, automatic reference generators can accidentally use other dates for the publication date so make sure you thoroughly check the details in the reference.
- Is the information ordered correctly in the reference? The formatting of a reference will change depending on the style you use and the main four styles are outlined in the next section!

Key Point: After you finish your work, you need to check it for any missing citations using the steps above.

CITING AND REFERENCING WITH THE HARVARD STYLE

Within the Harvard style, there are a few rules to use depending on the type of resource and the number of authors. Below, you will find a handy guide that you can refer back to throughout university, addressing every citation situation you will come across, with both narrative and in-text citations:

- Citing when there is 1 author

  Note, the author's name and year of publication are separated by a comma. Additionally, the sentence grammar (like the full stop!) will come after the citation.

In-text citation:

A recent study demonstrated the positive effects that Christmas trees can have on celebrations (Smith 2021).

Narrative citation:

Smith (2021) demonstrated the positive effects of Christmas trees on celebrations

---

- Citing when there are 2 or 3 authors
  If there are two or three authors, you should include all the authors' surnames in the citation. Typically, work with three authors will not be cited with a narrative citation.

In-text citation:

A recent study demonstrated the positive effects that Christmas trees can have on celebrations (Smith, Harvey and Johnson 2021).

Narrative citation:

Thompson and Farrel (2021) demonstrated the positive effects of Christmas tress on celebrations.

- Citing when there are more than 3 authors
  If there are more than 3 authors, you should use the abbreviation 'et al.' in your citation. You will notice that part of this phrase is a full stop, but you still put a comma to separate the name and the publication year.

> In-text citation:
>
> A recent study demonstrated the positive effects that Christmas trees can have on celebrations (Lampret et al. 2021).
>
> Narrative citation:
>
> Lampret et al. (2021) demonstrated the positive effects of Christmas trees on celebrations.

- Citing 2 different works from the same author in the same year
  To distinguish between the works, you add a letter after the year of publication. The two citations are always separated by a semi-colon. In this unique circumstance, in-text citations are typically used rather than narrative.

> In-text citation:
>
> A recent study demonstrated the positive effects that Christmas trees can have on celebrations (Nunan, 2021a; Nunan 2021b).
>
> Narrative citation:
>
> Nunan (2021a; 2021b) demonstrated the positive effects of Christmas trees on celebrations.

- Citing a direct quotation

    If you are using a direct quote from a source, according to the Harvard citation style you must use single quotation marks, not double. In Harvard style, double quotation marks are for quoting direct speech, rather than written literature and other sources. For direct quotes, remember you must also include the page number where you found the information! In this style, the year of publication and page number is separated by a colon.

In-text citation:

'Christmas tree sales were double this year compared to last year's purchases' (Claus 2021:p.24)

Narrative citation:

Claus (2021) stated that Christmas tree sales were double this year compared to last year's purchases (p.34).

- Citing an image

    An in-text citation should be used for any illustration, diagram, or image that you use in your text. You should treat these as if you're writing a citation for a direct quotation.

In-text citation:

Table demonstrating UK Christmas tree purchases per city in 2021 (Claus 2021:p.34)

Key Point: Different types of quotations require different citation formats.

After you have written your citation(s), the next thing to do is write your reference(s). Remember, this is a list of all of the sources you have cited in your assignment. If you are writing your references by hand, you should try to collect as much information as you can about the source, including:

- Author or editor – note up to 3 names
- Full title of the source
- Name of publisher
- Volume number (if applicable)
- Issue number (if applicable)

- Date of publication
- Page numbers (if applicable)
- Journal article title
- URL (if citing a website)
- Date of access (for online material)

- Research database identification number, for example, PubMed ID

When you write your list, it should be in alphabetical order, according to the surname of the first author or editor listed. If you have used more than 1 source that is written by the same author, then you should list the works in date order (not the order you use them in your work!) with the most recently published source first.

Here is a breakdown of how to structure a reference for a journal article, a website, and a book. Please note, only the author's surname, the first word of the title and any proper nouns should have a capital letter! The guides are written with only the words substituted in for a real reference, so you should italicise anything in italics and follow the grammar laid out:

- Journal: Author surname, initial. (year) 'Title of article'. *Title of journal.* Volume(Issue) Pages
- Website: Author surname, initial (year) *Title of Website.* Available at URL: insert URL (Accessed: date)
- Book: Author surname, inital (year) *Title of book* (Edition if not first edition.) Place of publication: insert place Publisher.

Key Point: A reference needs to contain information for a reader to be able to find a source from your citation.

CITING AND REFERENCING WITH NATURE STYLE

The Nature style is used prolifically in scientific writing and in many ways is much easier than other citation styles. To make a citation in Nature style, you need to write a superscript number where you want to make a citation:

> In-text citation:
>
> I want to place a citation here[1]

The next citation should be numbered 2, and so on. These numbers correspond to a reference marked with the same number in the reference list. As such, the reference list is ordered as per appearance in the work.

Here is a breakdown of how to structure a reference for a journal article, a website, and a book. Please note, only the author's surname, the first word of the title and any proper nouns should have a capital letter. The guides are written with only the words substituted in for a real reference, so you should italicise anything in italics and follow the grammar laid out:

- Journal: Author surname, initial. Title *Publication Title* Volume number, pages used (year)
- Website: Author surname, initial. Title. (year). At <insert website URL>
- Book: Author surname, initial. *Title*. Pages used (Publisher, year)

Key Point: Nature citations require a superscript number that refers to a corresponding reference.

CITING AND REFERENCING WITH APA STYLE

The APA style is a 'word-date' style, just like the Harvard style. Citations can be narrative or in-text (see Avoiding Plagiarism chapter and the Harvard section above). The citations are very similar to the Harvard style, except in APA, you should add a comma between the author surname and year of publication when writing in-text citations. The other difference is the use of 'et al.' – in Harvard, you must use this for more than 3 authors, however in APA, if a source has more than two authors, you may use 'et al.'.

There are also some minor differences between the reference formats. Here is a breakdown of how to structure a reference for a journal article, a website, and a book. Please note, only the author's surname, the first word of the title and any proper nouns should have a capital letter! The guides are written with only the words substituted in for a real reference, so you should italicise anything in italics and follow the grammar laid out:

- Journal: Author surname, initial. (year) Title of article. *Title of journal, Volume*(Issue) Pages. https://doi/insertDOI
- Website: Author surname, initial (year) *Title of Website. Insert URL (Accessed: date – only if the website is designed to change regularly)*
- Book: Author surname, inital (year). *Title of book* (Edition if not first edition.) Publisher. https://doi.org/insert DOI

> **Key Point:** Beware! APA and Harvard referencing styles are very similar but with key formatting differences.

LITERATURE REVIEWS

Almost all students never encounter literature reviews until they are at university, so if you have no idea what a literature review is, you are not alone! Literature reviews should be conducted before any significant work assignment, like an essay, academic presentation, or dissertation. A literature review involves you searching and evaluating the existing literature of a given subject area and accomplishes three things:

- Provides an overview of all literature in a given, specific area
- Presents the existing literature in an organised way
- Allows for critical analysis of the existing research in a given area, for examples, shows areas in need of further research and demonstrated limitations of existing theories

As such, a literature review summarises the existing body of research and can justify why you have focussed on a particular area. Building on existing knowledge is an essential element to research and if you don't do a literature review, you are at a high risk of repeating existing work or creating work based on outdated information. If you're conducting a research project or experiment, a literature review can also help you design methodology and approach the data in the way typically accepted by the field.

Key Point: You must do a literature review before starting any original research or significant piece of work. It is also good practise to do one before any work assignment!

WHAT MUST A LITERATURE REVIEW INCLUDE?

A literature review must be a comprehensive summary of the established knowledge base in a particular subject area and an up to date synopsis of current theories. It isn't an overview of the whole subject, but a background to a specific research question. The literature review should also outline the strengths and limitations of both the knowledge base and current ideas and opinions.

A literature review is structured like an essay, with an introduction, main body of text, and conclusion, however, unlike in essays, there are some things you have to address in each section. A literature review introduction typically contains an overview of how your literature review is structured (the layout of your essay). You should also define your topic by clearly stating what you are reviewing or investigating, and if necessary, include details about the place, time or persons you are studying. You also must provide a justification for completing a literature review, which in most cases, can be to provide a summary of up-to-date literature and identify under-researched or developed areas. Lastly, you must define the scope of your review, which means setting out the limits to what you will and will not evaluate, and why. Defining the scope of your review is a really important step, as it justifies why you haven't taken into account particular factors and describes your perspective of the field or concept that you are reviewing. As such, be very clear and direct with your language. For more information about academic styles of writing, please see the Academic Writing paragraph.

The main body of the text is comprised of summaries of the literature that was found in the literature search. This should be organised in themes and can be structured with sub-headings. Many students try to write as they read, meaning that they don't first gain a good overview of the literature search results. This is obvious when reading the middle of their literature review as the organisation and structure is often poor. As such, it is vital to plan out the literature review and logically organise the main body. The strengths and limitations of the evidence should also be evaluated here.

Lastly, the conclusion should summarise the key points of the existing literature, summarise any flaws or gaps in the existing body of evidence, and outline the areas for future study. The conclusion should also explain the links between the results found in the literature review and your own research proposal. Students are always surprised about the length of university conclusions compared to the conclusions they have written previously for their school work. A literature review conclusion can be over one page, so don't be concerned that you're writing too much!

> **Key Point:** A literature review looks like an essay, but you must include specific points in each section.

HOW TO CONDUCT A LITERATURE REVIEW

1. Your literature review should be guided by a question – remember, a literature review isn't a review of all the literature to do with a field rather, it provides context for a specific research question. Your question shouldn't be too broad or too narrow and because of its goldilocks nature, it can take a long time to write a question. If you are conducting a literature review for an original piece of research, try to get as much feedback as you can on your question and scope – this can be from your supervisors, from peers, or from specialised search librarians.

2. Decide the scope of your review. This means setting the boundaries of what you will evaluate and providing a rationale for these boundaries. Boundaries you may want to consider include
   - Time range: you may use all research that has ever been published or examine a particular time-frame or year.
   - Population: unless your work will be a global assessment, you usually can limit your literature review to a relevant population, for example, children or the UK. You can be as specific as you want – for example, a stipulation could be that your population has a certain occupation or attribute.
   - Number of studies to consider: your time is a finite resource, so you may stipulate that you will randomly select a certain number of studies.

3. Next, you must select the databases you will search, including libraries, electronic databases or internet searches like Google Scholar. Make sure you use reputable databases, so guidance from search librarians or your research group can really help with this selection. You may choose to use only one database or multiple. If you use more than one database, you should make sure you delete any repeated work in your results. For more information about how to conduct a literature search, see the Academic Searches chapter. Make sure you keep a record of your searches in case you need to duplicate them later or submit them with your work.

4. Once you have conducted your search, you should review all of the returned research studies. Consider examining the bibliographies and reference lists for any relevant studies that may have been undetected by your search.

5. Review the literature. You may find thinking about the following questions helpful:
   - What is the study's research question?
   - What methods are used in the study? Does the methodology have any flaws or limitations?
   - Do other studies included in the literature review contradict the findings of this study?
   - Has this study been cited? If not, why?
   - Do the authors have any conflicts of interest or funding sources?

> **Key Point:** Setting the question ands cope of your literature review is the most crucial step to shape your literature review.

THINGS TO REMEMBER

As stated above, the structure of the literature review is key. Students often subject reviews with poor structures or illogical thematic organisation, which demonstrates that they did not conduct their literature review properly. Taking time to read through the literature and organise it, really pays off in your finished product. Students can feel overwhelmed when they are reviewing the results of their literature because there can be over 100 articles to read, evaluate, and organise. To help organise the literature into logical categories, some students use post-stick notes with the source title on it and place them under sub-headings of themes. As students read further into the literature from the literature search, an organisation scheme can become clearer, and the post-sticks enable you to move sources around from topic to topic.

One of the most common mistakes students make whilst writing a literature review is describing the literature. It is very easy to shift your perspective from evaluating the literature to describing your results. To prevent this, you should periodically take a step back and review your work. Be critical and don't be afraid to rewrite passages if your style drifts into description rather than evaluation. Refer to the questions in point 5, above. These can guide you to ensure you evaluate the literature instead of describing it.

The main thing to remember as you write your literature review, is that it can take a lot of time and organisation to synthesise a good quality literature review. Many students view a literature review as something they need to tick off for their assignment, and forget that the review shapes the entire end product of their work, be it an essay, dissertation, or even a thesis. The time you spend writing a literature review also can save you time whilst writing your work assignment, because it is an unparalleled exercise that gives you an in-depth knowledge of all literature relevant to your project.

> **Key Point:** A good literature review can take a lot of time to complete, but remember, it's worth it in the end!

MANAGING SOURCES EFFECTIVELY

Usually, a good academic literature search or literature review can yield around one hundred (or more!) literature items. The sheer number of sources can be difficult to manage and without a system or managing tool, you may miss vital sources out from your citations or even just lose track that they exist!

VIRTUAL SOURCE MANAGERS

Thankfully, there is plenty of online software that can help you manage these citations. Before you pay for a subscription, check out the free software from Mendeley and Zotero. Your university will also probably have a subscription to EndNote or other software that you can use – just ask your librarian for details on how to use the university subscription. Each software has a slightly different user interface but offers very similar functions, usually including:

- Automatic citation downloads and insertion
- Automatic reference and bibliography generation
- Manual reference editing

Note, sometimes you have to download extra plugins to use all of the citation software functions, but these plugins are usually free. Relevant plugins can include word processor plugins (to insert the citations into your text) and web browser plugins (to download the reference). Some citation software will also synchronise your citations with an online 'cloud' server so you won't lose them if your computer crashes or fails. Try to pick a citation software that has this service (usually free from Mendeley and with the EndNote subscription), because in the unlikely event your laptop fails you, you know you have the literature you have amassed, saved and accessible.

Citation software is great because it automatically changes the numbering of the citations and references if you insert more citations above. However, you must always check your reference because the auto-generate can sometimes make big mistakes, like identifying the website URL as the reference, rather than the online book you are accessing. Many students have lost marks and changed degree award boundaries because of this mistake, so although autogenerated citations and references can save you a lot of time, you must always check them through and edit them as necessary. More information about how to recognise well written citations and how to correct citations can be found in the Avoiding Plagiarism and the Fundamentals of Referencing chapters.

If you are unsure about which referencing software to use, or how to use different functions, your library service will have a dedicated librarian who can help with source management and are great resources!

> **Key Point:** Source management software can save you a lot of time when using multiple sources but always check the references before submitting your work!

MANAGING PAPER LITERATURE SOURCES

Often, students studying humanities subjects will use a mixture of sources available online and sources that are not available online. Usually these physical sources are books or records of some sort. As discussed before (please see the Fundamentals of Referencing and Avoiding Plagiarism chapters), some students choose to reference as they write, which makes keeping track of physical sources much easier. However, most students write and then reference, so to avoid plagiarism and losing track of sources, many students use sticky notes. Students mark the places where they have sourced information or quotes by tagging it with a sticky note and writing on it where in their own original work they have inserted this citation. This is essentially creating reverse citations! Please note, you must be careful of old books when using sticky notes by using notes that contain neutral adhesives or by slipping in pieces of normal printer paper instead.

After you have created these reverse citations and written your assignment, you then go through the notes you have left yourself and insert the citations in your body of work as necessary.

Key Point: It can be difficult to keep track of physical sources whilst writing long assignments. Mark what you have used so you can go back to it later and insert the citation within your body of text.

EFFECTIVE RESEARCH

During university, a part of your course may include time to complete a research project, which may be examined, or you may choose to get involved in academic research in your spare time. Regardless of your subject, being part of a research group is a great opportunity for you, and one that you probably will not be able to access after you leave university. Taking the initiative to get involved in research beyond your course classes demonstrates your time management skills, ability to work both in a team and independently, and will give you some experience of a professional environment. However, taking on extra research can be a lot of work and may detract from your performance in your course studies, so you must continually reflect on your workload so you don't burn out! Furthermore, it should be noted that getting involved in research is often unpaid and on a voluntary basis, but you do get the chance to learn research techniques, get involved with publications or conferences, and gain vital experience for your CV.

HOW TO GET INVOLVED IN RESEARCH

It can be difficult to get involved with research to start with, but once you have a project or relationship with a research group, further opportunities are quite common. If a research project is required for your course, the course administration will often send around a list of potential research groups you could contact and inquire about joining. Alternatively, some students can contact laboratories and groups independently.

Each research group will have a special small area that they focus on, even if they are part of the same division or department. For example, a division could be Tudor England Research but you can have groups within this division studying their own topics within Tudor England, like women's fashion or International Policy. Some groups can even be more specific, studying smaller topics like foreign policies related to French relations or the use of lace in Tudor times. If you are looking for potential research opportunities, the best thing to do is find a division that is focussing on things you are interested in.

Then, look at the descriptions and information provided of each group in that division. This information is usually on the division website under 'Research Groups' or 'Current Projects'. Once you have found a group that interests you, email the Principle Investigator (PI), which is the official title for the group leader, with your university email. You should include your CV in the email (please see Preparing for Post Graduate Study for more information on how to write a CV) and what sort of project you are looking for – this can be data based or lab based, short term or long term. You may find that you have to send out a lot of emails before you get a positive reply, so much like job applications, don't be disheartened if you never hear back from the PI.

> **Key Point:** Do your research before you write to a research group leader! Find out what they study and see if it interests you or aligns with your long-term goals.

TIME MANAGEMENT IN RESEARCH SETTINGS

Unless you are taking on a research project as part of your degree course, you will be undertaking this research at the same time as managing a full class load. Each class load and student are difficult, so there is no single optimal schedule or way to split up your time between classes and research, however, there are several things you should consider when you're managing your research time and producing a research timeline:

• A start and an end date	You should have two end dates in mind. The first end date should be a rough, ideal date that you would like to end by but know you may have corrections or final jobs to complete after this date. The second date should be a concrete, unmovable date, after which you do not want to have any outstanding new work to do for the project. You may want to consider your course work or exam dates when deciding this second end date. It's really important to have time allocated for your main, non-research priorities!

- Timing of experiments

You will often have to submit a rough timeline of your research and experiments to funding sources and the research division. If your research will take place in a laboratory, some experiments might have to run over several days. This means you have to start them early in the week in order to avoid working on the weekends. Check with your supervisor if your department allows weekend lab work and schedule around your other commitments! If you have to wait for the beginning of a week to begin some of your work, this can delay your project or you may want to reorder your experiments.

If your research uses archives or data that can only be accessed in certain places, familiarise yourself not just with the opening hours but also any restrictions related to access, like photocopying rules or special collection availability. These rules may push back or restrict your access by a couple of hours, but over the course of your project, it may push you back a few weeks!

- Pause periods

You may want to build in 'pause' periods, where you have a predetermined and agreed time for a break from your research project. Most students will take these breaks for times when they know their course work load will be high, but it is also important to build these pause periods into your timetable so you can have some time away from your research! Time away can benefit your work too, by giving your perspective and a fresh mindset.

- Catch up time

Many students do not put in catch up periods into their timetables or schedule and sorely regret it. Catch up time is time that you schedule, in anticipation that your schedule will run over. These blocks of time can be used like 'extra time' in sports events, to finish up what you need to do. This takes away the stress of being behind your schedule and the pressure to find time to make up the work.

Key Point: Make sure you have a reasonable and clear idea of the time you have available for your research project.

HOW TO CONDUCT RESEARCH: GOOD COMMUNICATION

During your research project, you should actively try to foster a good working relationship with your supervisor. Key to this is open communication – you must keep your supervisor updated with your progress and be honest about things you are struggling with. You will find some guidance about how to productively communicate in the Effective Communication chapter. Your supervisor is essentially your boss in the research lab, but they are also there to support your contributions to the research group. As such, if you keep them updated about problems you have then they may be able to help you problem solve, preventing more wasted time! It is also important that you are honest about the time you may need for tasks and if you are on track. Being behind in research is frustrating but it is not unreasonable. If you maintain an open channel of communication and ensure everyone is on the same page, then a lot of issues and pressure can be avoided!

Sometimes students can find their supervisor can be a bit demanding or unreasonable with deadlines. Most often this arises from lack of communication between the student and supervisor, as the supervisor doesn't know about the other demands the student is juggling with the research work. A demanding supervisor can be really frustrating and stressful to deal with, but try to be professional and calm when speaking with your supervisor.

Don't struggle on and work unreasonable hours to meet their demands – set up a meeting with them and speak to them about your work load. To make the conversation productive, come to the conversation with a rough idea of the pace of work or specific deadline you will be able to manage. Beware that your supervisor may be under deadlines themselves to get this work finished or published, so you may have to compromise on your time frame. That being said, you need to define limits for yourself for what you can reasonably achieve in the time given and make sure your research project doesn't become a cause of unreasonable stress.

> **Key Point:** Good communication is essential to form a good working relationship with your supervisor. It can also minimise stress and conflict.

HOW TO CONDUCT RESEARCH: DOCUMENTATION

The next section will discuss general stages of research that you should be aware of and will probably have to conduct during your project! As each project is different, you may find that some steps are not necessary for your specific work, but it's important for you to understand each process so you can justify why you don't need to include it in your project. Before we cover these steps, it's important we cover a general housekeeping note for all research which is documentation. Every single step in your project should have notes, labels from laboratory kits, protocols, and other key documents. You need to save every single one for the future – either in one notebook with each page dated and signed or in a file on your laptop. Document everything – experiments that work and experiments that didn't! Even things you think you won't include in your final manuscript. You may need to hand over these notes when you leave the lab.

Many students find that they are included in publications years after they leave a research group, because of experiments and notes they made in the lab book, and handed to their supervisor at the end of their project. These notes also serve as records that might be submitted to funding sources to show how your group has used the funding. Additionally, these notes will help you when writing up your project, especially if it's a long-term research goal!

> **Key Point:** Throughout your project, you need to keep dated documentation of each step you do for legal purposes but also for your own benefit when writing up!

HOW TO CONDUCT RESEARCH: IMPACT ASSESSMENTS

Impact assessments should be performed to help confirm your research question or project focus. Sometimes, impact assessments may even identify a new area that you may not have considered focussing on. As a university student you are most likely going to contribute to smaller parts of larger projects run by full time researchers, and if this is the case, you won't need to perform an impact assessment.

Impact assessments can estimate the effect your research may have on the scientific field and on society in general. Impact assessments can also be used to assess the impact or burden of taking part in an experiment, similar to a risk assessment. These assessments are unlike any other piece of academic work so we have provided a rough guide so you can familiarise yourself with how to perform an impact assessment. Your group may have a set protocol or checklist for your impact assessment, so check with them for old copies or drafts that you could refer to when creating your own!

1. Describe your project

   Try to briefly outline three things: the context of the field before your project will occur, a description of what your project is, and lastly, the changes your project will make to the field and wider context.

2. Determine the key differences (or impacts)

This is arguably the most important step of your impact assessment and involves comparing the field or wider global context before your project and the expected changes that you will see after your project. Make sure you consider both large and smaller changes within your field in and in a wider context! Some students find it useful to brainstorm these changes with other researchers or peers to get a broad range of perspectives and ideas! You may also consider including significant things in your field that will not change with this project, similar to defining your project scope.

3. Describe the effects of the impacts listed in step 2

For each item listed in step 2, write out potential side effects caused by this change. You may also want to acknowledge key changes that will not have any impact. You should also attempt to write a strategy to monitor for these side effects and prevent them from happening. Some students find it is helpful to write this step in a table, with four columns:

Impacts (from step 2)	Potential Side Effects	How to Monitor for this Side Effect	How to Prevent this Side Effect
Difference 1...			
Difference 2...			

4.	Sorting	Order your potential impacts in order of probability to occur. If applicable, you should take into account any costs and the effort to make this impact happen. It is impossible to use generic guidelines to measure or estimate the probability of specific impacts in a given field, and so here is where your supervisor and research group can contribute and support your work.
5.	Decision making	Use the list you made in step 4 to create a document with potential impacts – both positive and negative – and how you may mitigate them. You should also compare the benefits of following your monitoring and mitigation plans compared with not acknowledging the potential impact.

After students create their impact assessment, they are often unsure about what to do with their results. You should discuss your assessment results with your supervisors and other research group members. The question you should answer in these meetings is what you should or shouldn't do in response to the impacts you have identified:

- You may change your entire research question, if a desired impact seems unlikely with your current project or intervention
- You may alter your experiment design
- You may do nothing about the impacts you have identified. Remember, sometimes doing nothing, is doing something!

> **Key Point:** Impact assessments can be difficult to do without any other feedback or input, so don't be shy – reach out to friends, fellow researchers, and your supervisor for their opinions!

HOW TO CONDUCT RESEARCH: SITUATING THE FIELD

If your research project forms part of your dissertation or thesis for your university course, you must include a section where you situate your project and yourself within the research context. This step is rarely explained when you are writing up your work, so this section will give you some guidance about how to approach it!

The first task is to provide background justification for why you chose to do your project as you did it. This may include a justification for your topic studied, the place or population you chose to focus on, and the direction of your project. Some students can have quite personal reasons for their choice of project and it is acceptable to include your personal experiences and motivations. This is seen most often in social science orientated projects but is accepted in the majority of written works.

The second task in situating the field is to describe your position in the project. This doesn't mean listing off what you personally did and thought up, but instead defining your situation in the research. When a researcher conducts an experiment or observational assignment, they can be inside and/or outside of the experiment. For interventional experiments, if you are inside the experiment, this implies that you are in charge of initiating the experiment and also conducting the research. If you are on the outside, you are separate from the research setting and don't have any involvement in the research intervention or aims. For other projects, inside/outside situations can also describe how you are personally attached to the project. Situation and perception of situation is something that only the researcher can identify for themselves and define, however we have provided an example below to better illustrate what personal situation is in research:

- The researcher is a student who identifies as Chinese, grew up in Canada and attends a university in the UK. This student is researching the farming practices of rural Chinese villages.
- This researcher feels like they are inside because they speak the same language as the participants and identifies as Chinese, as do the participants

- This researcher could consider themselves outside because they are not from a farming background and also attend a university (that is in Canada).

Key Point: Throughout your project, you need to keep dated documentation of each step you do for legal purposes but also for your own benefit when writing up!

HOW TO CONDUCT RESEARCH: EXAMINER REQUIREMENTS

If your research is part of your university course, you may need to submit something from your project to be graded or examined. In some universities, research projects can account for over 50% of the final grade, so it can be a really important part of your course! If your research project will be assessed you must make sure you are really familiar with the examination requirements (also called conventions), that your course sets out, preferably before you begin your project. If you don't have access to your examination conventions, email your course administrator as soon as possible!

Many students don't familiarise themselves with the course examination conventions, putting themselves at a major disadvantage, because the conventions are essentially your mark scheme, and you should tailor your project and write up to the mark scheme. Many students think that they need an amazing and brilliant project with great results to get a good grade, but this isn't true. Most exam conventions will outline the areas that you need to cover to get a good mark in your project, focussing more on the process of research rather than the results you get! Lots of things can go wrong or run over time, especially in laboratory or archive based research and the examiners know this, so won't base marks off of successful results or significance of the work. You should keep the exam conventions in your mind any time you need to make a research decision or need to allocate time to different tasks.

Once you have a good idea of what you need to achieve to get a good mark in your project, make sure you communicate this to your supervisor. They may not be familiar with your course or the mark scheme, and your supervisor can be a great resource to steer you in the right direction. It also will facilitate a good working relationship between you and your supervisor, because everyone will be on the same page regarding what you want to get out of the time you're in the lab – and your supervisor will tell you what they want to see from you during your time too! Lastly, you should ask your supervisor and research group to read through your course work before you submit it to your professors. It's common practice to provide them with a copy of the exam conventions to guide them, but more than likely they will ask you for a brief overview of important marks you need to hit! If you can give them a few concise bullet points to work off of, it can save both of you time and enable constructive criticism that is relevant to your mark scheme.

Sometimes, your supervisor's priorities may clash with your priorities or what the exam conventions say. This is most common at the write up stage of your project. It's important that you remember and respect that your supervisor is a really experienced researcher, but also bear in mind that examined work may not have the same layout or goals as a normal research manuscript. Most students and their supervisors solve this problem by having two versions of the manuscript – one for your course examiners and one to publish in an academic journal. This seems like extra and pointless work when you're stressed about your project submission to your examiners, but most students find writing the academic journal manuscript really good preparation for any verbal examined conversations you may have based on your research.

> **Key Point**: Familiarity with exam conventions will allow you to tailor your work to gain the maximum possible marks for your work!

HOW TO CONDUCT RESEARCH: GOOD CLINICAL PRACTICE

Good clinical practice (also referred to as GCP) is an international standard that all clinical research should meet. Good clinical practice involves both ethical and scientific quality, which aims to provide rigorous data from studies whilst also protecting the rights and wellbeing of study participants. As such, it's a very important element of all clinical research and every member of the research group has a responsibility to make sure the research being conducted abides by and considers these rules. You will also undertake good clinical practice training relevant to your research before you start the project. These are free and available to NHS and UK universities online. As a student in a research group, your supervisor can help you make sure that you don't miss out on any training or key guidance – don't worry, you won't be solely responsible for ensuring good clinical practice!

> **Key Point:** Good clinical practice must be the centre of any clinical research as it functions to protect participants and produced valid data.

HOW TO CONDUCT RESEARCH: EFFECTIVE ANALYSIS

When you have collected your data, whether it is from a laboratory experiment, a database, or from archives, you need to make sure you analyse it effectively. This is because data analysis is the process in which you turn your raw data into conclusions.

Before you being your research project, you should write a protocol of methodology in which you have outlined how you will analyse the project data. To do this, you need to understand what type of data your project will produce, and which method, including which statistical tests (if applicable) are appropriate to use. You should never produce the data and then decide how you will analyse the data, as the shape of the data or contents can potentially introduce bias into your analysis, therefore, your conclusions.

Project data can generally be split into two categories, quantitative and qualitative:

- Quantitative data: This data is measurable. This means that you can count it, relating to numbers. Quantitative data can provide investigators with causation and relationships with factors.
- Qualitative data: This data is descriptive and observational. Generally, this data cannot provide any insight into causation or relationships between factors, so no judgements between factors can be made.

Because of the differences in data types, quantitative data and qualitative data must be analysed in different ways. Statistical analysis can be applied to quantitative data, and it can be presented in tables, graphs and figures.

In contrast, you cannot apply statistical analysis to qualitative data, instead you need to perform content analysis. This analysis aims to understand the meaning of the data and can sometimes classify the data so it can be presented in a systematic way. There are many types of statistical analysis tests and content analysis methods, and some strategies will be more appropriate for your type of data. Make sure you ask your supervisor if you need help to pick what type of analysis you should run. Almost all students (and some researchers!) at some point struggle to understand what type of analysis they should do in their experiments. The first step is always identifying the type of data that will be produced (either quantitative or qualitative). This first step is something that you should be able to do independently. After this, you should choose a specific test and discuss it with your supervisor. They will be familiar with the type of data you produce and may be able to offer some feedback (or just encouragement!) about the analysis you should run.

> **Key Point:** You need to plan your data analysis strategy before you run any experiments! Ask your supervisor or research group for support so you use the optimal analysis method.

HOW TO CONDUCT RESEARCH: ACADEMIC RIGOUR

The phrase 'academic rigour' is used a lot throughout university – from courses and classes to research, but when students are asked to define it, lots struggle! Rigour is a measure of research quality and so the control of bias, validity of results, and dependability of data all contribute to scientific rigour. Rigour in quantitative studies and qualitative studies is approached slightly differently. In quantitative studies, rigour can be achieved by designing a good protocol that contains bias control measures, randomisation, blinding, repetition, and appropriate data analysis, where applicable. The second step to quantitative rigour is the investigator strictly sticking to the predetermined protocol that was written before the experiment started. It's important that you report your rigour when writing up your research, for both course work and for journal publication. As such, when you write up you should also aim to be as transparent and detailed as possible, so your process and research can be replicated and understood clearly.

In qualitative studies, the nature of the research means that rigour requires more than sticking to a good protocol. Instead, a rigorous qualitative research must also be achieved by staying within the boundaries and focus of your research question and scope. Due to the nature of qualitative protocols, rigour is often also accompanied by trustworthiness. An investigator can establish trustworthiness by transparency, good scientific communication (for example, a detailed methodology), and good academic practice by including citations.

> **Key Point:** You should try to make your research as academically rigorous as possible – from planning your experiment to writing up your work with transparency.

HOW TO CONDUCT RESEARCH: ETHICAL RIGOUR

Every research study must be ethically rigorous. This means that the investigators must be honest in what methodology they use, the data they produced, and the way they use the data. Poor ethical rigour can include manipulation of data to fit preferred conclusions and fabricating (making up) data. These two examples represent two different levels of poor rigour: manipulation of data is a crafty deception which if discovered, will lead to your publication being redacted, a fail grade for your course project, and potentially expulsion from your university. However, if you make up data or your data analysis, then this is research misconduct, which in some cases can be a criminal act of fraud.

You must never manipulate your findings or fabricate data. In most cases, researchers are genuine professionals who perform ethically rigorous work and will only tolerate ethical practice from their colleagues and students. However, if you do witness poor ethical practice, you should speak to your academic supervisor or a member of faculty that you trust about it.

Key Point: Ethical rigour in research is unnegotiable and you should always be confident that your data and conclusions are true representations of your research.

HOW TO CONDUCT RESEARCH: A FINAL NOTE

For any student, starting a research project is a really busy time. There are a lot of things to consider in planning your specific project but also many things to do to ensure you are researching responsible, as described in this chapter. On top of this, you may also be meeting a lot of new people and perhaps familiarising yourself with a new building or area. Starting a new research project is a really exciting time but make sure you take a step back and take time for yourself, so you can perform at your best!

Every student is different, and you may adapt to research quickly or may need some more time. It can be quite difficult to communicate that you are struggling but it's really important that your supervisor or someone you trust knows about it and can offer you support. Even the most impressive research supervisors and professors have struggled, so they will be happy to help and make sure you're in the right place so you can thrive.

PRACTICAL ASPECTS OF RESEARCH

Before university, some students may have observed research groups, but usually, university research projects are students' first time actively doing research. Actually 'doing research' is a unique task that no other experience can really prepare you for, and until you have stood at a lab bench or been into archives to collect data, it can be difficult to appreciate this! In this book, we have covered research concepts you should consider during your research project (Effective Research chapter) and how to write up your manuscript (Publication chapter), and this chapter will cover the more practical aspects of day – to – day research. One of the most exciting (and nerve – wracking!) times for a university student is starting in a new research lab or doing research for the first time. You probably don't know what to expect but you naturally want to do well and have a good time! This chapter aims to help familiarise you with what to expect (and what to do!) in your research lab or archive. It will be useful to read this chapter before your first day!

YOUR FIRST DAY AT THE LAB

Before your first day, make sure you have contacted your supervisor about where and when to meet them. Every research lab will require access cards or codes to access because the computers will contain sensitive data and there may be controlled chemicals in the lab. Arrive early so you can navigate these doors or get your access card from the security office. As a last note on access cards that students are never told – remember to bring your card with you to the toilet and lunch room or you may get stuck between card access doors or outside the lab. Every person will forget their card once and will never do it again! Most people keep their card on a lanyard so they don't get caught out.

Usually on your first day, your supervisor or a lab member will give you a tour of the building and lab. You will not be able to bring any food or drink inside laboratories, but usually lab members will leave their water bottles just outside the door – make sure you have named yours.

Lastly, try to sort out your access cards, codes, and computer logins on the first day. Bring an official photo identification document with you on the first day as it is usually required for approval to lab areas. It takes a while for them to be processed and it can hold up your research, so be proactive, even though it's a really boring task to do!

RUNNING EXPERIMENTS: PLANNING YOUR EXPERIMENTS

So, you've settled into the lab and now you're about to start your first experiment. This section will take you through how to conduct experiments with good methodology, which is a skill that will be applicable throughout your research career.

Once you have defined your research question, the next step is to plan your methodology, which is how you will investigate this question. On a blank piece of paper, write out the project question and aims, so you can visually refer back to it through your planning process. Now, ask yourself what data will be needed to answer this overall question and how you will get this data. This will probably be the end experiment that will ultimately answer your question. After you have figured this out, you need to then ask yourself what data do you need to back up this experiment or solve any assumptions you may make. These experiments will be run first to provide a foundation of evidence. After running these experiments, it may be necessary to change your last experiment, depending on the data. An example is:

- Research question:

  Does regular counselling sessions improve mental health and academic results amongst undergraduate university students.

- Ultimate experiment:

  A two-group experiment with group 1 receiving regular counselling sessions and group 2 receiving no counselling sessions.

  This experiment will measure mental health wellbeing through regular surveys and mental health assessment through psychiatric tests like the mini mental state examination. Academic success can be measured through university exam results.

- Information to enable the ultimate experiment to happen:

1. Define the average baseline mental health of university students. This could be done by surveys or assessments by licenced psychiatrists

2. Define what 'regular counselling sessions' are – do these have to be similar for every student receiving them?
   To work this out, I might run an experiment to see the effect of standardised counselling sessions versus personalised counselling sessions

3. I want to see if I can find out why regular counselling sessions do or don't improve mental health and academic results. To do this:
   I could ask study participants for their opinions.
   I could perform a meta-analysis of the literature focussing on the effect of counselling sessions
   I could run brain imaging and medical tests to determine if there is a biological reason why counselling sessions were or weren't effective. These tests should happen before the participants enter the ultimate experiment's process and after to see the effect of the counselling sessions.

Unless you are investigating a brand-new concept (something that you may do as a postgraduate researcher), your research group will have a good grounding in the relevant experiments or areas that you will use. Make sure you get feedback from the research group before starting because you may have to collect data or run experiments that might answer the last questions in your project before you run your main experiment!

> **Key Point:** Make sure you have a clear idea of what experiments you need to run in order to answer your research question.

RUNNING EXPERIMENTS: PRACTICING GOOD METHODOLOGY

After you have written out your methodology and determined the order you should do your experiments, you are ready to start your practical research! As a university student, you will work fairly independently on a day- to -day basis and it can be difficult to know how to start!

The first thing to do is to print out the methodology and read through the protocol for the experiment you want to do that day. Read it from start to finish and highlight any key steps. Things to pay attention to include:

- Time periods where you need to wait for the experiment, like incubation steps.
- Specific measurements like temperatures, volumes, and concentrations
- Machines you may need to use like water baths or centrifuges

These details are really important, as you need to follow the protocol exactly, in order to conduct a rigorous and reliable experiment. If you don't follow the methodology steps precisely, your data will be unreliable and unreproducible (unless you state these deviations in your methodology write- up). Next, clean down your bench so you know it isn't contaminated with anything.

Then, make a list of all of the equipment you will need before you start as you may need to borrow equipment from other people and some steps may be time sensitive (so you won't have time to rummage around for a special pipette!) Lay out this equipment neatly. At this point, ask your supervisor to show you how to use any machines you need during the experiment. You may need these machines later on, but you never know when your supervisor will be around to show you, so grab the opportunity whilst you can. Don't be embarrassed about writing down the instructions or taking photographs or the display screen – do whatever you need to do to ensure you are able to properly run the machine!

Now, put on any personal protective equipment you need, like gloves and goggles, and gather all the 'ingredients' you need for the experiment. Measure out quantities and concentrations before you start (if possible). Usually, you should use plastic 'boats' to measure solids out – keeping each ingredient separate and unspoiled. Liquids can be measured in clean flasks or tubes.

After you do this, read through the protocol again to make sure you know exactly what you're doing. Keep this on your bench so you can refer back to it throughout your experiment.

Now, you are ready to start your experiment. Make sure you keep exactly to the protocol and ask your supervisor if you've not sure about anything. It's always better to clarify than to guess and your supervisor will respect you for making sure you are conducting the experiment properly. If you deviate or change the protocol (or make a mistake!) you should tell your supervisor because it changes the experiment you are running, and could influence the results. Remember, rigorous academic work is achieved by following your carefully designed protocol to the letter, so take your time and make sure each step is correct. Tick off steps when you have completed them and make sure you keep good documentation (see the Effective Research chapter) of whatever you do, including any mistakes or deviations you make.

> **Key Point:** Thoroughly knowing your protocol and preparing your lab bench well can help you run your experiments correctly and with academic rigour.

RUNNING EXPERIMENTS: DAY – TO – DAY TIME MANAGEMENT

Although you will already have a good idea about your overall project time scale, you should also plan your time on a day- to – day basis. Lots of students don't do this, which means that they use their time inefficiently and don't complete their experiments that day. Usually experiments can't be left overnight, so it's really important you have a clear plan of your time. In order to plan effectively, you should read through the protocol for an experiment and then plan your day based on the tasks you need to achieve. Take note of any time gaps or 'waiting times' in your protocol and try to schedule your lunch break around these gaps! If you don't have a good chunk of time where you can leave your experiment, try to find a logical place to take a break in. You may not have one in your protocol, and if that is the case, just try to work out how long it will take you to complete each step and take a break in between steps where lunchtime logically falls. Although it might be tempting or seem necessary, never skip your breaks or lunchtime because you need the time to refocus your mind to give you the best possible chance of following your protocol accurately and not make silly mistakes!

Another time management aspect that students don't really get told about is to do with longer experiments. Sometimes, experiments may run over a few days or you may need to grow things for a few weeks before you use them. This means that you may need to work over weekends. If your experiment runs over a few days, try to schedule it for the beginning of the week so it doesn't overlap with the weekend, however, if you are growing things, like plants, then coming into the lab to water them might be unavoidable. If you work over the weekend, make sure you still get two days break off from the lab. You can't work 24/7 and you need to take time for yourself! Be professional and ensure you communicate this to your supervisor, for example, "I have to come into the lab over the weekend for a few hours, so if it's ok, I will come in on Monday afternoon instead of the morning. I've planned out my time so it works with my experiments'.

Key Point: Plan out your day in advance, making sure it fits well with your experiments for the day!

ARCHIVE RESEARCH: DAY – TO – DAY TIME MANAGEMENT

The first step for efficient time management in archive research is finding out when the archives are open. Take special care when looking at opening hours for weekends and bank holidays, as archives tend to shut early or be completely closed.

Apart from the archive opening hours, if your research is archive- based, you have complete control over your day – to – day time management, similar to when you are revising for exams. You can find strategies for time management that are completely transferable to archive research in the 'How to Revise' section. Whatever strategy you choose to follow when working in the archives, it is important to make sure that you take regular breaks. Usually archives are located in rooms with little natural light and fresh air, so try to go outside for short walks or to eat your meals. Uniquely, archive research is really tempting to work until late hours or until you have finished a certain section. Ultimately, this is unsustainable for your entire project, so try to be strict with yourself from the start of the project and have a clear time where you stop work and go home to relax. Some students find it useful to create a time-log instead of a timetable, which details what they did retrospectively, rather than projecting tasks to complete the next day. This means that you can keep track of your work whilst not feeling guilty about not finishing everything on your to-do list.

> **Key Point:** Archive research time management requires you to actively decide when to take breaks and stop working – remember your research is a marathon and not a sprint!

COMMUNICATING METHODOLOGY

Your written methodology must be an accurate and true report of what you did during your research (see the Publication chapter for more information). If you are not truthful or accurate with your methodology, your work is not academically rigorous, and your data may not be reproducible. As such, it is really important to write up your methodology accurately and clearly. To help this, whilst you run your experiments or conduct your archive research, you should always take good notes and document what you have done (please see the Effective Research chapter for guidance on documentation). When you write up your methodology, you should always consult these notes to see if you did what you said you did, and if not, how you deviated from the protocol. Changes to protocol must be recorded and also written in your manuscript methodology.

When writing your methodology, use short sentences so your meaning is clear, and include as much information as possible. Your methodology should read as a list of instructions that anyone can follow to reproduce your experiment. This means you should include measurements, concentrations, and chemical manufacturer details, for example:

- 2mL of 35% hydrochloric acid (Chemitect and Co. Batch number 039)

If your work is archive based, you should also write out your methodology clearly and accurately. This means you should publish your search strategies, your criteria for including literature in your search, and use citations (please see the Fundamentals of Referencing and How to Avoid Plagiarism for more information about citations and references).

Remember, your methodology should be written without interpretations or discussion about what you did. It should read like a recipe or a list of instructions. After you have written up your methodology, you should always seek feedback from your supervisor and research group as they will be experienced in manuscript writing. Some students find it helpful to use their methodology and pretend to run the experiments again, to see if they have included enough detail.

> **Key Point:** The principle aim of the methodology section in your manuscript is to clearly and accurately detail your methods to demonstrate academic rigour and enable others to reproduce your work.

COMMON RESEARCH PROBLEMS

Even if you practise your methodology perfectly, there will be times when experiments don't work. For many students, this can be the first time that something hasn't succeeded and may not be able to be solved by thinking it through! The first step to tackle this problem is always reviewing the protocol and methodology to see if you can identify a step where you made a mistake. If this doesn't work, you might have to just re-do the experiment and hope for the best. If it still doesn't work, ask your supervisor or a senior research colleague to watch you run the experiment to make sure you're doing it right. It can be really frustrating, especially if you have no idea where things went wrong, but the most productive way to solve the issue is to systematically go through the experiment and methodology to see where the problem lies. Try to remember that everyone makes mistakes and you can only do your best!

Sometimes, there are points in experiments or archive research when you just don't know what to do next. Here, you may be completely reliant on your supervisor and you may have to wait for them to help you. When you're stuck at this point in an experiment, it can be really frustrating because you probably know what you need to do *after* this specific point, but you just need to get advice on this specific step! To avoid this happening, make sure read through the protocol and ask your supervisor any questions you have in advance or make a list of questions to ask your supervisor when they are in the lab!

If you don't take advantage of their physical presence, you will have to email them and wait for a response.

Another common problem is waiting for equipment or experiment ingredients to arrive. This is frustrating because you have no control over the delivery time and may be held up in your overall project. If this happens, see if you can reorder the experiments and do what you can do at the time. You may also be able to start writing up your manuscript during this time, especially the introduction or methodology. If you really can't do anything and must wait for the delivery – take the time off to relax (but remember to ask and inform your supervisor!) It can require some experience and maturity to be brave and realise that there is nothing to do, but if there really isn't anything you can do, take the time to have a break so you can come back to the lab re-energised and with a fresh mindset.

Key Point: Research can be frustrating at times, but try to productively solve your issues and remember that your supervisor is there to support you!

READING LISTS

At university, some courses and professors will provide a reading lists, containing relevant books, articles, and other academic works. Reading lists can either be course-wide, so relevant for the entire course, or specific to a work assignment. They can be any length, from a couple of titles to hundreds of books, and so just using a reading list can be a lot of work even before you tackle your academic tasks! Whilst you read the items on your reading list, you must remember to take good quality notes to use for your work – please see the Understanding Research Papers for tips on how to approach and take notes on research literature.

Reading lists are helpful because they can point you in the right direction for reputable evidence and current opinions. Some students critique reading lists because they lead you in the direction of what the professor thinks is important, rather than enabling you to create original thoughts and ideas, however, this is untrue! It is absolutely vital to understand the existing literature in order to make reasonable, novel conclusions. In this way, you can think of a reading list to be a ready-made literature review – but be aware that it may not contain all the up to date literature your own literature search would. Some professors may not update their reading list for smaller new developments in the field, so conducting a brief search for other material can be useful. For more information and guidance about literature searches, please refer to the Literature Search chapter.

It's important to note that you should not buy every (or any!) book on your reading list. These will all be available through the university library for you to access for free. If your reading list is short, it can be beneficial to reserve the books as soon as possible to ensure you have access to them (please see the How to Use Libraries chapter).

Key Point: Reading lists can help you find relevant, academic information for your work or course.

USING READING LISTS WITH A LEARNING DIFFERENCE

If you have a learning difference, reading lists can be quite daunting. Reading lists should never become an obstacle to your learning or have a negative impact on your mental health, so seeking learning support early is crucial. The key thing to remember is that reading lists are designed to help guide you to useful literature. Your professors haven't written one and sent it to you simply to torture you with hours of unproductive reading! Be proactive and support your learning by talking to the professor and asking them to highlight a few they would prioritise.

If you are known to the university's learning support services, ask your learning adviser for suggestions to make your reading list more manageable. Your adviser may even add strategies to your unique learning plan, for example, some students receive smaller reading lists or summaries of some works to help them navigate a longer reading list. Others can qualify for longer deadlines.

If you don't feel comfortable approaching your professors or the university support services, talking to peers or students in the years above for their advice can be very useful, but also intimidating. Remember, asking peers can be easier than asking experts and professors, but their help will have more limitations.

> **Key Point:** Some students can find reading lists to be impossible and stressful. Ask your adviser for support if you need it – don't struggle needlessly!

HOW TO USE A READING LIST – LONGER LISTS

Longer reading lists are usually course-related lists, rather than for a single assignment. These reading lists can be over one hundred items long and so managing a long reading list is all about organisation and prioritisation. They can be organised by topic, by author, or by type of publication. You should read list items according to subject, so organising your long reading list into topics can save you a lot of time long term. If your list is not digital, even colour-coding the items will help! You may be able to judge what the source is discussing from the title, but sometimes it requires you to quickly read the introduction to sort it correctly.

At the beginning of university, almost every student thinks that they need to read every single item on their reading list. If your list is long, this is an impossible task and you shouldn't attempt to do it! Don't be intimidated by students who broadcast that they have read the entire reading list – it is highly unlikely that they will meaningfully remember a lot of the sources they may have read. Remember that the aim of a longer reading list is to give you a broad view of the subject – this can be achieved by reading a few select texts from a variety of topics within your reading list. As such, selecting and prioritising texts to read is an important step! This means, if you start reading a source and it echoes similar views to another you have read, put it down and move on to the next – you can always come back to the source after you have finished your other priority reading items.

Whilst you read, make notes on the paper or book (please see the Understanding Research Papers chapter) and keep them in a dedicated place for your reading list. That way, all your reading list notes are in one place and can be easily referred to throughout your course. You may also choose to annotate your reading list with a short summary of the text, so in the future you can quickly find relevant literature.

If your reading list is for your thesis or dissertation, reading the majority of texts in the list will be necessary. Here, you must pace yourself and take good quality notes so you can remember and refer to what you read (please see the Understanding Research Papers chapter, which offers some guidance for note taking from research papers). Lots of students, even at postgraduate level, feel a lot of pressure from reading lists and stressed that they haven't covered every aspect of a topic. One way to tackle this is to create multiple mini lists from your main reading list. If you have 100 items on your reading list for 'colours', select 10 that represent the broad topic and start there (pick a rainbow of colours!) then add another 10. Chunking a big task like this, instead of reading all 10 papers on the colour red, means that you haven't compromised range of knowledge.

> **Key Point:** Longer reading lists require organisation and prioritisation. It is worth dedicating time to figure out your priority reads!

HOW TO USE A READING LIST – SHORTER LISTS

The strategy to approach a short reading list (with less than approximately 10 suggested items) is much simpler than a longer reading list (over 10 suggested items). Each item on a short reading list is there for a reason – there usually isn't much redundancy or lighter reading included. Instead, each item usually represents a vital, unique piece of information or perspective. As such, it is often necessary to read every item on a short reading list. Sometimes, reading the whole reading list is impossible, for example if you have a learning difference or a short deadline. Whenever you are trying to selectively read items from a reading list, you must make sure that you read a range of sources that will give you a good overview (not just from one perspective!) of the subject.

This might be difficult to tell until you start reading the items, so don't be afraid to stop reading what you previously chose or just flick through it quickly. In these cases, you may also want to prioritise reading the shorter items such as journal articles or book chapters. By prioritising shorter items, you can read more works and absorb more perspectives on the topic than reading one complex textbook.

> **Key Point:** Some students can find reading lists to be impossible and stressful. Ask your adviser for support if you need it – don't struggle needlessly!

TACKLING READING LISTS WITH TEAMWORK

Some students form study groups to tackle coursework, including reading lists. These study groups can be brilliant resources as each person will bring a unique perspective and interpretation of texts. Some students can have bad academic experiences with these groups if some team members fail to complete their tasks, resulting in an uneven workload, but the majority find it an efficient way to work. You should also be mindful that each student will have their own view of each source, so you may not agree with their interpretations and conclusions. If you decide to split a reading list between a group, make sure each person has a range of texts to read – that way, if someone fails to read and provide notes for their set, then your group won't completely lack knowledge of a specific topic. Make sure you set a clear deadline for your group and ensure everyone knows how you are going to share your notes with each other.

> **Key Point:** Taking a team approach to long reading lists can be really useful but also has its drawbacks – decide carefully if you want to use this approach!

WHAT TO DO IF YOU DON'T HAVE A READING LIST

For some courses or work assignments, you may not be provided a reading list. It can be strange adjusting from having a reading list to not having that indirect guidance from your professors, but don't panic! You could conduct your own literature review (see Literature Reviews chapter), or you may want to start off by reading through your lecture notes and finding any references your lectures make to literature. Normally, the last slide of the lecture print-out will be a slide full of references. You can then use the reference section from these articles to guide you towards what next to read, and go on from there.

At university there can be a lot of emphasis on individual performance, and so students can feel very isolated when tackling work assignments, forgetting the rich network of support around them. If searching for literature isn't yielding good results, email the professor who set the work assignment and ask for their reading recommendations. Alternatively, ask your course mates or friends who are in the years above for any tips.

> **Key Point:** If you aren't provided a reading list, you can always create your own!

COMMON READING LIST WORRIES

> *"Everyone on my course has read more than me"*
>
> Almost every student will worry about this at some point during university. This worry may even be true if you haven't made much progress with your reading list. It's crucial to remember that although reading lists are designed to give you a broad view of a subject, it is how you use this evidence and work within your own work, not how much you have read that counts!

"My reading list is so long it seems impossible"

Remember to chunk down larger reading lists into manageable portions. Make sure your chunks feature a variety of source topics so you don't leave any topics unaddressed in your reading!

"An article in my reading list is contradicted by another, what is correct?"

Sometimes the sources included in your reading list contradict each other, or contradict other sources that you have found external to the list. Firstly, you should check if one of the publications is a correction or advancement from the other. An easy way to do this is to check the publication dates and then searching to see which view other authors have supported. It may be that the 'right' answer isn't known and you have just found two separate

"I'm in the middle of my reading list and I can't face reading another journal article"

Take a break – it's marathon not a sprint. Emerge from your reading nook and get some fresh air and natural light! Students can often shrink their

ACADEMIC WRITING

This chapter will give you an overview of all the different types of academic writing that you will encounter during university and help you improve academic writing skills. It's important to note that academic writing is a skill that you will develop throughout your time at university and regardless of how good your academic writing is for your first assignment, by the end of your degree you will see a huge improvement between your first and last few assignments!

If English isn't your first language, you may feel that writing in an academic style is a big leap from your conversational language skills. Many non – native English speakers can feel disadvantaged compared to students for which English is a first language, however, academic writing is difficult for all students as it's a skill rarely practised at school level in the UK. If you are an international student and find you are particularly struggling with your academic writing, universities often have workshops and classes to support you adjust to the style of writing. It's very common to use these university services to support the transition to UK university life. You can contact the international students' rep or your professors as they will know how to access these classes.

TYPES OF ACADEMIC WRITING

There are multiple types of academic writing, all of which you will author yourself during university! It is important to know what type of source you are reading or writing, because they are all formatted differently and are written for different purposes! It is usually straight forward to recognise different types of academic writing once you are familiar with the different styles:

- Essay — A self-contained case answering a question (usually set by a lecturer), that justifies arguments made with evidence from sources.

- Research paper or article — A written report of original research carried out by the student

- Thesis

  In the UK, this typically refers to a long project write up that is completed by a PhD student.

- Dissertation

  In the UK, this typically refers to a medium length write up of work completed for a bachelor's or master's degree

- Research proposal

  A written plan outlining future research. This can be required when applying for funding.

- Literature review

  An evaluative synthesis of existing literature or research on a specific subject area, answering a specific question.

- Lab report

  A write up of the aims, methods, results, conclusions and discussion of a laboratory experiment.

Key Point: There are lots of different types of academic writing to be familiar with.

WHAT IS AN ACADEMIC STYLE OF WRITING?

Overall, the aim of academic style writing is to accurately convey information. As such, in any subject, the primary academic writing should clearly provide information without bias. Crucial to academic writing is that any argument or conclusion is supported by evidence, which should be cited and referenced. This evidence must be an accurate account of the source and presented impartially.

Beyond the overall aims of academic writing, the style has a formal tone, but aims to be read easily. Sentences are kept short and although technical terms may be included in academic writing, these must be defined for the reader. Even if the technical language appears to be straight forward, it is important to define them as the definition provides your perspective and use of the word. Academic writing should be well-structured to increase the clarity of writing.

Typically, writing is split into sub-headings, but within paragraphs and sections, your points should develop logically. This can allow the reader to follow your points and understand your overall argument.

Lastly, academic writing is written passively and so it doesn't include 'I', 'they', or 'you'. This is something many students struggle with at first, but is something you can easily get used to doing. Occasionally, it can be impossible to write in the passive, and in these cases, you can use 'we' to refer to yourself or any other investigators. If you want to refer to other work, you should use a formal citation (please see the Fundamentals of Referencing) and use 'the group' to refer to them, if necessary.

> Key Point: Academic writing is a formal but clear style of writing that you will develop throughout your time at university.

HOW TO WRITE IN AN ACADEMIC STYLE

This section will guide you through how to approach writing in an academic style. It's important to remember that academic writing is a skill that you will continue to develop throughout your time at university and beyond – it isn't something you will immediately learn. Students often find referring back to the fundamentals of academic writing helpful in reinforcing and evolving their own academic writing skills.

- Defining your purpose

  One of the most important things to do in all academic writing is framing your work. This means clearly defining the context of your writing and the purpose of your writing. Students can find it helpful to think of this as setting out the 'problem' and how their work will address this 'problem'. This is generally very clear in research, but if you're tackling an essay or dissertation, it can be more difficult. Spend time to interpret your question, as this framing will set the course for your whole essay and arguments. An example is:

It is estimated that there over 300 million people worldwide with type 1 diabetes[1]. More than half of patients in rural South-East Asian do not have access to glucose monitoring kits or diabetes services. Poor glucose control can increase risk of developing complications secondary to diabetes[2], including diabetic retinopathy[3-7]. Here, we investigated the effect of diabetes education and free access to glucose monitoring on the incidence of diabetic retinopathy cases in rural South-East Asian communities.

This is a very concise example of how to frame your work, however, the example contains both the 'problem' and how this work will address this 'problem'. You can see that the 'problem' is backed up with evidence, cited in Nature style, which is common for scientific papers. Many students find it difficult to fully illustrate the 'problem' and set up the premise for their work. A trick you can use is to work backwards from your work and ask: what assumptions are needed to justify my work? You can highlight key words like so:

Here, we investigated the effect of <u>diabetes education and free access to glucose monitoring</u> on incidence of <u>diabetic retinopathy</u> cases in <u>rural South-East Asian communities.</u>

After you have identified key words, you need to justify why the key word is a problem that needs solving and collect some evidence for this. If you're studying a particular element of a disease or problem, like here, you should also include some context of the general problem that is supported by evidence. Here, the evidence is, 'It is estimated that there over 300 million people worldwide with type 1 diabetes'. You should be able to link back each key word to sentences and evidence in your introduction, framing your research!

Key Point: Creating a context, or frame, for your work is an important step in academic writing.

• Structuring your work

Academic writing should be logically structured. The strongest academic work always has a strong and clear structure that progressively builds evidence to support your conclusions. Some students skip this stage and fail to map out their work, which leads to convoluted arguments, confused reasoning, and poorly supported conclusions.

To structure academic work, you should always consider two structures at once:
1. The overall structure of the work
2. The structure within a paragraph or the point you're trying to convey

Academic writing is most often structured with an introduction, which primarily aims to define your purpose (see above!), a main body, and a conclusion. It can be difficult to structure the main body of text because it can involve composing several distinct concepts or ideas into an argument that supports your single conclusion. The main consideration when structuring the middle of your piece of writing is to make it easy for the reader to follow and understand. This will differ depending on the subject, the writer, and of course, the reader! Don't be afraid of tweaking the order of your paragraphs as you write to see if another order is better!

The structure within a paragraph is also important and must be considered at all times when writing. Never begin writing if you do not have a clear view of what you want to say! Some students view a paragraph as a miniature essay – with an introduction setting the scene, the 'middle' that develops the point or concept, and the end ties up the paragraph in a summary. If your paragraph is complex, try to write it in these three distinct sections to ensure you have a very clear framework. A good test to use after writing a paragraph or section, is to summarise what point you were trying to make in one (or two!) sentences. Read back through your work and see if you have achieved making this point by the end of the paragraph.

Signposting your structure is invaluable to the reader. Make it clear when you have moved on to a different point, or if you are adding more arguments to support the same concept. We all want to believe that someone reading our work is devoting their full attention to it, but in reality, that's not the case and signposting your structure can reinforce the structure and your overall messages. Words like:

- However
- As such
- Furthermore

- Consequently
- Firstly...finally
- Additionally

can be really useful to ground the reader and make your work easier to follow. This is because words like this can demonstrate the sequence of your thoughts and arguments.

Key Point: Never start writing unless you know exactly point you want to make – and why!

- Incorporating evidence

Throughout this book, you will find endorsements for using evidence to support your work. Whilst adjusting to university, almost every student will find this to be a difficult skill to gain and use confidently. There are several methods to employ when you want to incorporate evidence (from other people's work!) into your own. The most common are quoting and paraphrasing. Remember, it is absolutely vital that you include a citation wherever you have used a source in order to avoid plagiarising (see Avoiding Plagiarism and The Fundamentals of Referencing chapters for further guidance).

Most students struggle to incorporate evidence into their work so if you're finding it difficult, don't panic! Your work shouldn't be a patchwork of external sources, but instead also use quotes and paraphrases to support your own ideas and interpretations. In scientific writing, quotations and paraphrasing are rare, but you may use it to provide background information or to frame your own work. An example is:

'Lorenzana (2019) previously demonstrated native communities of people meet several boundaries to healthcare. As such, our results may be skewed...

This sentence summarises an entire journal article's findings and provides evidence that supports an original interpretation of data. This is a very brief example and you may wish to provide an overview of Lorenzana's work, but the sentence is also sufficient.

The same principles apply to humanities subjects and the social sciences. Here, the evidence you use may be direct quotes from literature, interpretations from other researchers, or evidence from multi-media sources.

Women in Wuthering Heights represent wild and tamed with examples of Catherine and Isabelle, respectively. However, this presentation is limited by the era and social expectations Bronte wrote in, as both women birth a child. Arguably, Catherine is unable to be forced conform to society's ideals of a good woman (Hurt, 1966), and abandon her nature as 'half-savage and hardy' (Bronte, 1847, p.35) as she dies soon after childbirth. Fatalism is further discussed...

Just remember, for any piece of writing you should use evidence to back up your ideas and correctly credit any external sources you use. With more practise, it becomes easier to embed evidence within your work so don't feel frustrated if you find it difficult at first – you will get better!

Key Point: All students struggle with incorporating evidence into their arguments and work. Don't worry, it will come with practise.

- Using clear and concise language

When writing in an academic style, you want to make sure you convey your ideas clearly to the reader. There are several common ways to ensure clarity of language including the vocabulary used and the sentence structure.

Firstly, include only one idea or concept per sentence. When you first start writing in an academic style, this means that sentences can seem too short but it is just the style of writing. Longer sentences can be difficult to follow, especially if you are discussing a complex idea. Your sentences should also follow a logical order, progressively forming an argument (please see the Structuring Your Work section).

The words you use in your writing have a large impact on the clarity of your work. At the beginning of this chapter, it is explained that you should avoid using words like 'I' and 'they', instead using 'we' if it is unavoidable. There are a few other 'word rules' that you should bear in mind when writing in the academic style. Academic writing is a formal style but not overly complex, so don't feel like you need to replace every word you may naturally use with a word from a thesaurus! However, words such as 'like', 'basically', and 'maybe' should be avoided as well as any clichés. Lastly, you should try to write words out in full, for example, write 'do not' instead of 'don't'.

Some departments or research groups favour using either the active or passive voice. It is technically correct to use both in academic writing, but you should check with your supervisor before you start writing!

The active voice makes the <u>subject</u> of the sentence in charge of the action:

- <u>Participants</u> completed the survey three times per week

Whereas the passive voice puts the <u>subject</u> at the end of the sentence, or even leaves it out completely:

- The survey was completed three times per week by the <u>participants</u> or
- The survey was completed three times per week

Generally, the passive voice is considered to be the most formal, but usually you use a mix of both the active and the passive in academic work. The only reason why you should stick to one type is departmental preference.

Key Point: Use short sentences to ensure your sentence conveys the meaning you want it to!

- Conveying your opinion

Within academic writing, you may be required to put forward your own ideas or conclusions based upon the evidence you have presented. It can be very difficult to do this in the passive voice, so below are some helpful phrases you can employ instead of saying 'I think' or 'I believe':

- This suggests
- This explains
- This is an example of
- This supports
- There is a strong case for
- As such

You should also be conscious of the verbs you choose to use in your writing – not all verbs are created equal! Generally, there are neutral and strong verbs, and you should be mindful about where you use both types of verbs. Strong verbs, such as 'argue', 'emphasise', 'reject', 'content', or 'refute', can be used if the evidence strongly indicates one particular conclusion. When using these strong verbs, it's vital that you are using them in the context of a good evidence base. More neutral verbs can be used throughout your essay, for example: 'demonstrate', 'describe', 'note', 'report', and 'show'.

COMMUNICATING COMPLEX CONCEPTS

Students often find it difficult to convey the complex ideas or links that they identify between concepts in their written work. Usually, there is a single paragraph or concept within an essay or dissertation that is tricky to write clearly.

If you come across this problem, first ask yourself: is this tricky to write because it needs other points and paragraphs to support what I'm saying here? If this is the case, repositioning this paragraph later in the main body of text may help. Sometimes, the tricky paragraph is difficult to write because it's actually better placed in the conclusion. This might be the case if your idea is too complex to unravel from other linking and supporting evidence. In the conclusion, you can much more easily refer back to previous points compared to how you would write a main body paragraph, solving your tricky paragraph!

Positioning and structure may not be the cause of your difficulty in communicating a concept. It could be simply because the concept is complex! Most students will continue to try and work a paragraph until it makes sense, but this can be counterproductive. Instead, you should create space for your mind to think clearly – some students use a completely new piece of paper, go to another place to work, or have a break away from the essay. Once you have established this space, it can help to write or speak aloud, your idea in your own words – however you most naturally would explain it. Some students find it helpful to write down the key word or concept they are trying to explain and making a mind-map about the word. The visual representation can organise your thoughts into a logical progression. After this, you can create sentences and change the wording into a more formal, academic language.

Diagrams and graphs can also be good way to explain complex concepts, by either adding colour to the written explanation or even replacing the written explanation entirely. Remember, you can add annotations to diagrams to further explain your points. Designing figures to help explain your point can take time and you may go through a lot of draft diagrams before you find the perfect one for you.

> **Key Point:** Use short sentences to ensure your sentence conveys the meaning you want it to!

ACCESSIBLE WRITTEN COMMUNICATION

There are a range of reasons why writing an academic assignment can feel intimidating and even overwhelming. If you struggle with reading or writing, it may be an indication that you have a specific learning difference, such as dyslexia. As awareness and assessment quality increases, more and more students are discovering they have a learning difference and are receiving support that allows them to thrive at university.

If you suspect you may have a learning difference, your learning supervisor or university learning support service could refer you to get assessed. Although many students will feel reluctant to be 'labelled' as such, it can be useful to be 'diagnosed' as it will enable you to access all the support services and even some funding, to empower you in your learning. Students will be given a unique learning plan designed to support your specific learning needs. Some plans can include:

- Extra time during exams for reading and writing
- Adapted text styles for easier reading
- Workshops or tutoring sessions to learn techniques for revision and day-to-day university work
- Printed lecture handouts for annotation
- Subtitles or captions for recorded lectures
- Equipment for studying, such as a Dictaphone or laptop software

Every student is unique, so the examples above are just general examples to give you an idea of what support you may be able to get at university. No guide, book, or video will be as good as a tailored assessment and learning plan by experts, so if you feel like you struggle with reading or writing, speak to your adviser about it. As such, this section won't contain any tips, tricks, or 'coping strategies', because the best thing for you to do is to speak to an expert about it and get personally customised support for your learning.

Key Point: If reading or writing academic work seems like an impossible task, you may have a learning difference. Talk to your advisers to make sure you are supported throughout university.

HOW TO EFFECTIVELY ENGAGE IN CLASS

University classes are fundamentally different to the lessons you will have received at school. At school, your teacher may ask you questions, ensure you're paying attention, and frequently monitor your progress. None of these teaching mechanisms are common at university level, instead, you are responsible for your own learning (as outlined in the *How is University Different from School* chapter).

Engagement is more than simply attending a class. It means that you are actively listening to the class, thinking about the content being presented to you, and even attempting to apply these concepts to other relevant material or problems. In some courses, especially humanities courses, engagement can also include critically appraising the class content. Overall, engagement in university class can be thought of as understanding, considering, and remembering information/concepts. This chapter will provide you with guidance to help you get the most out of classes at university.

Key Point: Engaging in class is a brilliant way to get the most of your academic university experience.

GENERAL WAYS TO ENGAGE IN CLASS

This chapter will give you tips for staying engaged in each type of class you may encounter at university, but there are some strategies that can be employed in all of them. Firstly, try not to wear very casual clothes to classes like tracksuits or leggings. It's good to be comfortable during class, but generally you will subconsciously associate these clothes with relaxation rather than productivity! At times, you may find you have a busy schedule and will turn up to classes in sports kit or clothes from another activity – so long as you generally stick to this rule it will help to engage your brain into 'active mode', rather than a more passive mindset. Other ways to prepare yourself for class include waking up at least 40 minutes before class to make sure you're properly awake for class. You should also make sure you are fuelled to learn – your brain needs energy to function! Small snacks like fruit, oat bars, or biscuits are good to have before lectures as they will make sure your stomach isn't rumbling but won't make you too sleepy to focus fully.

> Key Point: Prepare yourself for class – dress, sleep and fuel to succeed!

For all classes, consider putting your phone on silent mode or aeroplane mode. Then, remove all temptation by putting your phone in your bag! You will be amazed how often students intermittently scroll through their phone during class. The few minutes you miss from the class may not be crucial, but these few minutes will change your mindset and focus. It is much more difficult to put down a distraction and immerse yourself fully back into a class than enter the class environment and focus at the start of the class! Make sure you tell your friends and family that you're going into class so won't be able to answer – you will be surprised how understanding they will be! Most people can respect that you have gone to university to get your education and will easily respect what you need to effectively study.

For some students, being completely uncontactable for an hour is not feasible due to caring or other responsibilities. Most phones have 'do not disturb' modes that you can customise, so you could silence social media apps but still get calls or messages from certain contacts.

> Key Point: Entering a class and having an engaged mindset from the start is much, much easier than trying to re-engage during the class!

Many students have a class in which they find it difficult to stay awake. This isn't a sign that the student is lazy or not trying hard enough, often it's multifactorial. Contributing factors can include the time of day, the temperature of the room, the levels of light, and the subject matter! If you feel comfortable telling the professor leading the session, it can be very effective to speak to them after class about keeping the lights on or opening a window. No professor wants students falling asleep in class, so they are generally very receptive to this. You may find approaching a professor a bit intimidating, so you can also raise these things with the department or course organisers. Potentially the professor's teaching style might contribute to your difficulties to engage in the class. If this is the case, it is probably most productive to raise it at the course review at the end of the class module or with the course administrator.

> **Key Point:** Class environment can contribute to your levels of attention and engagement. Take responsibility for your learning and ask for any changes you need to make the environment more stimulating.

Lastly, the most important thing you can do to enable yourself to engage in class is to academically prepare. This may be more applicable for some class formats like seminars or debates, but can also be applied to lectures. Lots of students find that if they have a small amount of background knowledge going into a lecture empowers them to think around the subject and add on to their existing knowledge base. This helps to engage you because by doing this, you are actively considering lecture content and engaging your brain! Lots of students believe that they have to read everything about the class topic or even go through the lecture notes in great detail. This unrealistic idea of what preparation is can prevent students from even attempting to prepare for a class. It's really important to understand that preparing for a class can involve anything that adds to your understanding of the class. The approach most students take is to look at the class title and choose at least one part of the lecture content to read about. Even reading one page of a textbook or academic paper will give you a platform to ground yourself to during a class. It can be difficult to prepare for classes if you're feeling stressed or time restricted, but many students find that doing a small amount of prep (like a page of reading, as recommended above) can make them feel more in control and ready to learn. This is because they have actively done something to add to their learning.

> **Key Point:** Preparing for a class can help you engage and feel on top of your work!

ENGAGING IN LECTURES

You may have one lecture every few days or multiple lectures per day depending on your course. Lectures are typically 1 hour long, which may not seem like a long time compared to your school classes, but they are much less interactive, making engagement difficult. Some lectures are now delivered via online learning or are pre-recorded. Whilst this can be more convenient for some learners, other students find that it is easier than ever to zone out of a lecture!

There are several tricks you can employ during lectures to keep you engaged:

- Choose your seat carefully! Lectures are typically held in lecture theatres with one big screen or board at the front and stepped seating. Try to sit in a seat where your eye level is at the level of the screen so your neck and back is comfortable. Don't sit too high up and near the back, because the distance between you and the lecture will encourage you to lose focus. Sitting at a mid to near level in the lecture theatre will also make it easier if you need to ask questions.

- The lecturer may give you either lecture slides or lecture notes. The slides are usually a printout of the presentation whereas the lecture notes can be a bulk of information that supplies the lecture content. Although you may feel that you have all of the information through these handouts or a recorded version of the lecture, many students find that annotating these handouts can help them to engage in the lecture. The process of making notes about the lecture ensures the student understands the lecture content and allows them to make connections between hearing the lecture and the notes.

- Bring plenty of water to your lecture. If you find yourself losing concentration, a refreshing drink can really help you reset your mind back to the class. Plus, water is good for your body, so it's a great way to stay hydrated!

- Think about a question that the lecture content has provoked. You don't have to ask your lecturer; indeed, you may be able to answer this question yourself! But by formulating a single question, it means that you understand the material enough to know what you don't know.

> **Key Point:** Lectures will probably be the main method of course content delivery. Actively participating in the lecture, by taking notes, formulating questions, and being a part of the immediate lecture environment can help you engage and focus.

ENGAGING IN SEMINARS

Many students say that seminars are their favourite type of class because they are given the chance to discuss work assignments with other students and the lecturer. Seminars are also a smaller class type, typically with around 10 students and held in a more informal classroom setting. Seminars are a brilliant resource for you to test out your original ideas, gauge how well you're doing with the course content, and have some interesting discussions! To engage in seminars, it is vital to prepare for the class. You should look up the title or discussion points and prepare the work or reading before the seminar. If your lecturer doesn't provide any clues as to what the seminar is about, you should ask them to, so you can take full advantage of the class. Many students have one experience of not being prepared for a seminar and try to never turn up without prepping ever again! Remember, you can't discuss something that you have no knowledge of. Equally, seminars are a good time to get help with any concepts you're struggling with or to answer any questions you have.

> **Key Point:** Prioritise preparation for seminars, if possible as seminars provide high-yield time with an academic.

ENGAGING IN TUTORIALS

At some universities, particularly Oxford and Cambridge, you will be offered tutorials in addition to departmental organised teaching. Tutorials are classes with a professor in which you discuss a pre-prepared piece of work (a problem sheet or an essay) and can have a couple of other students in, or even be a one – to – one session. These classes can be really easy to engage in because they go into depth into a specific topic and have a very small class size. Preparation for tutorials is expected and important, but it isn't expected for you to enter the tutorial as an expert on a topic. A great use of tutorial time is to ask questions and learn about different interpretations or opinions surrounding the topic you're focussing on. If you really feel like you haven't prepared to the extent you want to for the tutorial, consider contacting your tutor to reschedule the session. Hopefully this little section has helped to alleviate any trepidation you may feel about having a direct discussion about academics with a professor.

> **Key Point:** You can ask questions in a tutorial or develop a deep discussion – use them for your learning!

ENGAGING IN CONFERENCES

Conferences provide a unique environment where anyone involved in research can mingle, listen to talks about novel breakthroughs, and present their own work. Conferences are exciting places where you can find inspiration and are a great opportunity for networking. However, it can be an intense environment partly due to the organisers often hosting them in a hotel, with presentations, food, and if applicable, accommodation all within a very short distance from each other. Conferences often have talks scheduled throughout the day and due to the exciting content, students often easily initially engage with the presentations. Most students find that they fatigue during conferences and lose focus.

You should view a conference like a marathon – pace yourself! Make sure you take plenty of breaks when offered and even try to go outside for some sunlight and fresh air. Consider what talks are relevant to your work and talks that interest you, and attend these as a priority. For the lower priority talks, if you feel ready to learn and focus then you can go to them, but if not, try another conference activity or take the time to rest. Within the presentations themselves, please see the lecture tips on effective engagement for further guidance.

> **Key Point:** Conferences can sometimes make you forget the outside world. Remember to take breaks to reset your mind, in order to get the most benefit from the experience.

ACADEMIC PRESENTATIONS

Throughout university you will be required to make presentations about your and other people's work. Some of these presentations will be marked and count towards your final grade whereas others may be part of scholarship or funding applications. As such, presentation skills are crucial to develop!

In academia, presentations can be either poster or oral presentations. These presentations can be in your classroom, an exam hall, or at conferences. Please see the Conferences and Posters chapter for more information about different presentation types. As a rule, oral presentations are more competitive to win, so if you have the chance to apply for either, you should always apply for an oral presentation. You will not lose out by doing this as you will be allocated a poster presentation if your application is not successful. Please note, guidance for poster authorship can be found in the Conferences and Posters chapter.

Presentations can be a significant source of anxiety for some students, so if you or someone you know is struggling with having to deliver a presentation, seek support. Your professors, educational advisers, and counselling service have all encountered this problem before and will be supportive. Your examiners, professors, and course leaders do not intend for a presentation to be an obstacle to your education or good mental health. If you are struggling with a presentation, seek support early so adaptations can be put into place without rushing or extra stress.

Key Point: You may be examined on your presentations as part of your course, or they may be part of funding applications.

PLANNING YOUR ORAL PRESENTATION

Most broadly, an academic presentation aims to inform an audience about your academic work. How to tell the audience about your work can be difficult, but you should think of it as telling a story. Like any story, yours will begin by setting the scene, describing the background of the project and the general context. After this has been established, you then narrate what your project did and the results. At the end of the story, you will return back to the wider view of the project and paint your project in the scope of the wider world. Because this story will be the foundation of your presentation, you should decide what your project story is before you write either a script or slides for your presentation. This story should give a clear and concise telling of why you did your project, what you actually did in your project, and what you found. A common technique students use is to make 5 – 10 large squares on a piece of paper and write out their project in the squares using a few sentences, similar to a children's story book. Make sure your story ties up or acknowledges any unanswered areas or next steps. This story will form the foundation of your presentation, so take your time editing it!

Your story board may look a little like this:

Slide One: Background	Slide Two: The Hypothesis
On this slide you should set the scene for your presentation. Make sure every premise or assumption is established here. See the Academic Writing chapter for more information for how to write an effective and established background story. It is most effective to have a figure on the presentation slide and for you to talk around the figure	Even if you have alluded to your research question in slide one, it is good practice to really emphasise your hypothesis. Write it out in full and dedicate a slide to it to ensure your audience fully understands your project

Slide Three: The Project

This slide can be used to explain your experiment(s). If you have multiple little experiments, consider creating a flow diagram figure to explain where each experiment fits into the wider project. Don't go into minute detail – just make sure the audience knows what techniques you used and why you chose them.

Slide Four: The Project

Use another slide to describe your methods if this will give a clearer story. Remember, don't flood the audience with details of your experiments – only give them the key features

Slide Five: The Results

Clearly present your results. More guidance for how to do this can be found in the text below!

You may also want to include a slide with study limitations detailed

Slide Six: Conclusions (and References)

This slide ties up the project. It can be really slick to use the figure from slide one and link your findings with the background.

Key Point: Try to logically structure your presentation to best tell the evolving story of your work. This structure will for the foundation of your

CREATING YOUR PRESENTATION SLIDES

After you have your story written, the next thing to do is to create your presentation slides. You can use your story squares to structure your slides, however you may want to make some small edits, for example splitting up one slide into two. Try not to radically change the order of your slides unless you think it will improve the story telling of your project. Most students try to cram as much information as possible on a slide but this is the opposite of what you should do. The fewer words, the better! If you do write information on the slide, it should be to emphasise your most important points, or to answer a crucial question that your audience may have. When writing, make sure the information is written in bullet point form and each slide has no more than 3 bullet points on.

Most student's introduction slide is their weakest slide, so on the next page we have provided a brief example of how to set up premise and assumptions on a background slide. Because you have to set up the background and justify the project, you may need to use more than 3 bullet points on this slide if you can't replace the words with a good diagram. Here, our example presentation reports the findings of a study investigating the number of princesses that need saving in fiction published from 1900 – present, and any correlation with ethnicity or date of publication:

Princesses 1900 – present

Princess Saving = When a female presenting character is placed in a situation of disadvantage she:

1. may be able to extract herself from with no or limited help from other characters, but does not attempt to
2. is rescued from this situation by a male presenting character
3. usually becomes romantically involved with the character in point 2.

For this slide, I would make the text defining princess saving appear after princess figure whilst I was talking:

'The presentation of women in literature often reflects the place and role of women in society at the time of writing. In this project, we investigated the number of princesses in fairy-tale literature from 1900 – present, who required saving in the story. We also looked at any correlation between rates of princess saving and factors such as ethnicity and date of publication. We defined princess saving as: (text appears on slide) the following....'

In this example, the picture of a princess is very basic and doesn't help to tell the story of the project, instead it focuses the audience on the topic and subtly indicates the underlying anti-feminist theme with the dress! To use fewer words, you should use figures or diagrams. Using figures correctly in a presentation is an easy way to elevate your talk and illustrate your concepts. A good presenter will use a figure by using the figure to support their talk, rather than describing the figure itself. A good figure can take a long time to make, so don't be frustrated if you have to dedicate a good portion of your presentation prep time to figure design. These figures can then also be used for a manuscript, if you later choose to publish your work in an academic journal.

Many academic presentations will use a central figure that describes the background and 'problem' the study is addressing as the first slide and the last slide. This way, the speaker can link the findings of the study straight back into the context and background that the audience has been familiarised with in the first slide. This can be a really effective summary and demonstrates the relevance of each finding. As with any academic work, try to get feedback on your figures, especially any that are central to your presentation, with plenty of time to edit. Remember, if you use figures or pictures from other sources, you must insert a citation to credit the author!

Although your presentation will be unique to your project, there are two slides that most researchers will format the same, the hypothesis slide and the results slides. This isn't because these two slides are the most important slide – in fact, in a good presentation all slides are essential and cannot be removed from the presentation without compromising the presentation story. The reason for formatting these slides like other presenters is that the hypothesis and the results slides must be exceptionally clear to the audience. The hypothesis slide is usually a slide with only the hypothesis written on it, with no other information. This means that the audience has the chance to devote their sole attention to your research question. Your results slides can be very simple too, with the finding written as a main statement, and any explanation, data, or figures placed under it.

Results

- **Fairy-tale princesses often need saving from a prince**

  89% [70 – 99] of all princesses included in the study required saving
  30% [20 – 49] of princesses from stories written after 2010 required saving

- **There was no significant difference in number of princesses needing saving from Caucasian and non-Caucasian backgrounds**

  60% [30 – 65] of Caucasian princesses versus 45 [30 – 80] of non-Caucasian princesses were found to require saving

  P > 0.05

HOW TO APPROACH PRESENTING

There are many ways to prepare for a presentation and over the course of your degree you will discover which strategy makes you feel the most prepared for your talk. Some students write out their presentation script in full and rote memorise it. After this, they will practise saying their script in time with their slides. Other students will have a note card with a few words on it to prompt them, but will speak about their project 'free-style'. The key element that unites any preparation strategy is that nothing is as good as standing up and practising saying your presentation in front of your teddy bear, family members, or friends. An old saying in performing arts is 'don't practise until you get it right, but practise until you can't get it wrong', and that is the best was to prepare for presentations, especially if you are being examined.

Remember that presentations are just like any other academic work assignment and feedback is key. A good test for your presentation is to see if your supervisor likes it but also if someone outside of your field can understand and follow it, for example, your family or friends. This is the ultimate test for your introduction because if you have successfully explained and set the scene of your project, anyone should be able to follow your presentation! Non-experts can also give you feedback about your speech style (remember not to talk too fast or too quietly!) and your body language, which should remain relaxed.

Many students find dressing for presentations to be another stressful element of a presentation! Wear something formal, for example a shirt and trousers or a smart dress, and make sure you are comfortable in it. The important thing is to be professional but comfortable! Try to avoid uncomfortable shoes or anything that may come with a risk of tripping over!

At the end of your presentation, there will be an opportunity for audience members to ask questions. You can prepare answers to obvious limitations of your project or your methodology. Practise answering those questions in front of a mirror and with friends or family. However, there may be questions you don't know the answer to and that's ok! You can always answer that 'that is an aim of future investigations' or 'currently this is unknown in the field', if that is true! Your research group can also support you by asking you questions, which usually will be harder than the questions you'll receive from those not in the same field as you and so are a great way to prepare!

> **Key Point:** Practise your presentation over and over again – it is the most valuable preparation you can do!

PRESENTING BEYOND UNIVERSITY

Many students find academic presentations stressful and fairly limited in their use beyond their degree. Although the format and content of academic presentations may not be so transferable beyond a university environment, academic presentations are a great resource to prepare you for interviews. Interviews are intense short periods where you need to be able to vocalise your thoughts in an organised manner and answer questions based on your existing knowledge base. Many students have said that experiencing this pressure through presentations and other verbal examinations really help their nerves and stress levels during real-life interviews. Additionally, many employers seek candidates that can present themselves and their views in a concise manner, and academic presentations form strong evidence that you can do this under pressure!

> **Key Point:** Skills you will learn from making academic presentations will be useful throughout your career!

CONFERENCES AND POSTERS

So, you've done a brilliant job and finished your research project – well done! The next step is to submit this project to a conference (nationally or internationally). Conferences are places where researchers can present their work and receive questions or feedback on it. Usually, conferences have a theme or area they will be discussing and so offer unparalleled opportunities to meet a diverse group of researchers working on similar or complimentary areas to your work. Here, you may find researchers with similar goals and offers for collaboration, creating new working relationships.

When you submit your work to a conference, you need to pick either an oral presentation or poster presentation. Oral presentations are often more competitive to gain and involve you making a short verbal presentation with slides. We will cover how to give an effective oral presentation in the next chapter. The requirements of poster presentations vary between conferences but they all require you to create a poster of your work. Your poster will be displayed in a large hall full of other posters and you stand alongside it to discuss your work with the conference attendees. It is important to know that once you present your work, you can't present it again unless it includes a significant update or novel development.

It is important to note that conference presentation submission and attendance can be expensive: a fee is usually required to submit your work, another fee is required to attend the conference, and then you need to consider travel costs! You should always ask your department or your university if there is any funding available for you to attend a conference. Another cost to conferences can be the cost of printing your poster – these posters are expensive to print as they are printed to the size of 1metre by 70 centimetres.

> **Key Point:** Conferences are a brilliant opportunity to present your work and receive feedback or offers for collaboration.

WHY YOU SHOULD SUBMIT YOUR WORK TO A CONFERENCE

Whether you want to pursue a career in academia or not, submitting your work to a conference is a great experience to interact with academics and junior researchers just like yourself. Conferences give you a chance to practise your communication skills and offers a chance to network with top researchers. Furthermore, creating a presentation can really help when you start to write up your project. This is because a presentation must have a really strong structure and strong storyline to convey the project from conception to completion. You can use this storyline as the basis of your manuscript!

If you are considering a career in academia, conference presentations are expected achievements to have at the time you apply for jobs. If you get a good opportunity to present your work, you should take it up, but don't panic if you haven't had the opportunity yet! There will be plenty of chances for you to present during your time at university. Preparing for a conference can be a lot of work at the end of a project, so it's important to weigh up the workload of submitting your project and the benefits for your career. Don't underestimate your fatigue and make sure you have an open and realistic dialogue with your supervisor about your mental fatigue and work load.

> **Key Point:** Submission of work to conferences comes at the end of projects, when you are most tired! Make sure you are in the right mindset to continue working rather than moving on to the next project.

HOW TO WRITE A POSTER

The first thing you should do when you're making your poster is research the dimensions and formatting requirements set out by the conference. These vary between conferences and it is much easier (and less frustrating!) to format the poster at the start rather than the finish! We recommend you create your poster in Microsoft PowerPoint because its interface for formatting and editing is well suited to the task. Usually, you can choose if your poster is landscape or portrait and your department will have a template that you can base your poster on. You should also ask your supervisor for the correct logos and emblems to use to acknowledge your institution and sources of funding.

After you have formatted your poster, you need to plan your layout – all posters will look unique, despite using similar templates. The minimum information you should include is:

- Introduction: This is to provide context to the areas you are studying. You can provide an introduction with this can be either in text form or through a figure that you can elaborate upon
- Hypothesis You must provide the question you are addressing through your work. This is arguably one of the most important pieces of information you should include and often researchers choose to put this in bold font or a different colour to highlight it. You may also include any secondary investigation aims.
- Methods Often a figure tells a thousand words! See if you can replace words with an image that can clearly tell the conferences attendees what you did
- Results This is another really important section so be prepared to devote a lot of space on your poster to present your results! Be diligent with the details on your figures and graphs as small misalignments can become major formatting errors when your poster is printed to size!

- Conclusion   This section is also important but often does not require as much space. It is crucial to clearly answer your hypothesis and investigation aims.

> **Key Point:** Formatting and presentation of your poster can make up the majority of the work load. To save time (and frustration!) make sure you correctly layout your poster before adding any information.

TOP TIPS ABOUT SUBMITTING YOUR WORK TO A CONFERENCE

- Ask your supervisor early about any conferences you could aim to submit your work to
- Make sure you know the deadline for submission and don't get caught out by different time zones as not all deadlines will be presented in GMT!
- You must submit your poster to your supervisor for a check over before submission. Make sure you have enough time to make any alterations they request.

You will be required to talk about your poster and project if an attendee asks. Please see the Presentation Chapter for more information on how to present your work well.

PUBLICATION

There are two main ways by which you can have your research published, either as a stand-alone independent manuscript or by having your work incorporated into a larger article with other researchers. This chapter will provide information about both processes, guiding you through to a publication!

Throughout this book, there are references to mindfulness and awareness of your fatigue levels whilst working. Writing up your project is no exception – this task comes at the end of your project and so it can be difficult to find the motivation to write up. Taking a short break between your project work and the write up can help you refocus.

> **Key Point:** Your work may be published as its own article or incorporated into a longer manuscript with other researchers' work.

AUTHORSHIP AND COLLABORATOR-SHIP

Whether you are submitting your work as a stand-alone publication or part of a bigger project, you should be aware that there are two ways of being acknowledged in a publication: as an author or as a collaborator. Authorship credits you for a significant contribution to the work, whereas collaborator-ship acknowledges a more minor contribution. Note that authors are not listed in alphabetical order, rather in order of contribution. If you are contributing to a larger project, you should ascertain what you will be credited with early on in the project. It is always much easier to know where you stand and to have open dialogue, rather than finding out last minute. Don't be scared to advocate for yourself if you believe you have contributed enough to be an author. It is usually best to do this face to face, but make sure you have a written confirmation for your authorship or collaborator-ship, just in case things are forgotten in the publication process – an email will suffice.

> **Key Point:** It is professionally accepted for you to find out how you will be credited in a publication. This conversation is usually best done face to face.

PUBLICATION COSTS

As a student you will not be responsible for most of the administration regarding publishing, including the fees associated with publication. Instead, your supervisor or group principle investigator will make sure these are paid. At this level, you should be aware that journals charge to publish your research and these fees can be very expensive. Your department or university will often cover publication and open access fees.

STAND-ALONE PUBLICATION

Congratulations! You've worked incredibly hard and are now ready to write up your project to submit it to an academic journal. The procedure to submit your manuscript will differ depending on the journal you are aiming for but the process of getting to the point of submission is fairly similar, regardless of project, subject, or journal.

Before you begin to write your manuscript, you should have a journal in mind to submit to. You need to make sure the journal you are targeting accepts your type of research – both topic and style of study – before starting out! Aiming for a particular journal will also allow you to write to the journal's preferred format (word counts and layout) rather than having to alter your work post-hoc.

There are hundreds of academic journals out there, so take advice from your supervisor and research group when choosing one. You may also consider 'impact factor' when choosing a journal to submit to. Impact factor is a measure of the journal's popularity and influence, with more prestigious journals having the highest impact factors. As a student, it is rare for your work to be published as a stand-alone article in a very prestigious journal, but it can happen! If you choose a lesser known journal to submit to, make sure that it is authentic by checking if it's endorsed or published on well-known research databases, like JSTOR or PubMed.

> **Key Point:** Impact factors is a measure of a journal's quality and how well-read the publication is.

HOW TO WRITE YOUR MANUSCRIPT

Once you have a journal you are aiming for, you can start writing up your project. The first step is to check for any requirements the journal may have, for example, word counts or figure limits. Some journals require a 'snapshot' paragraph of your project in addition to an abstract, so double check for any extra requirements! After this, there are no rules about how you should approach writing your manuscript! You don't have to write your article in a particular order and some people find writing the manuscript and then tackling the abstract the easiest approach. Lots of students struggle with how to distil their work into a manuscript, so below we have outlined key points to include in each section, no matter what your research focuses on:

- Abstract   The journal will have strict instructions about how long your abstract can be and what it must contain. Most abstracts must start by presenting the research context; what the existing problem is, in one sentence. Then, briefly outline what your project was with the key result(s). After this you need to summarise with your main concluding point.

It can be difficult to write a good, succinct abstract that fully presents the project's context and results. It can be easier to write your entire manuscript first and the condense that down to an abstract. That way, your abstract is consistent with the conclusions and themes in your manuscript. Please see the Understanding and Using Abstracts for some more information about how to write an abstract.

- Introduction

When writing an introduction, you must provide background to the main points that you raise in your manuscript. As such, if you are not fully confident with the research area you have focussed on, it can be easier to write the introduction after the discussion. That way, you can ensure that you include a logical explanation of all points raised in your manuscript.

- Methods

This is the easiest section to write! It requires you to write how you carried out your experiments, in so much detail that someone could read the method section and carry out the experiments themselves. This means you should include quantities, concentrations, and make of chemicals used. Think of this section as a recipe for your research project. Some students find this section the easiest to write, especially if their lab book or records are detailed. If you are writing your methods section and ask yourself if you are including too much detail, always remember that you can never include too much detail!

- Results

  Your results section must be written in a similar manner to your methods section – there should be no elaboration on your results. Instead you should just report your results clearly with no comments. Often, the results section is split up with subheadings to signpost each result and main finding. You may wish to include graphs or figures to illustrate your results further.

- Discussion

  In this section, you should interpret your results both in the context of the experiment and the wider question. You need to include an evaluation of the strengths and limitations of your study – usually this is done at the end of the discussion section. This section is hard if you don't understand the meaning or significance of your results. Ask your supervisor for help early on to get crucial feedback on the direction of your discussion

- Figures and Images

  You may wish to include images and figures in your publication. It is vital that you check the resolution range that the journal will accept and alter your images accordingly. Any images or figures you include should be accompanied by a number and title, explaining what the figure shows. You then use this number in the text to refer the reader to the image. Most students number their figures by inserting text boxes, but this means that you need to update every single figure by hand if the order changes. Some software has automatic numbering and labelling systems built in which can save a lot of time over your academic career!

- Supplementary or Appendix Data

With a short word count, it can be difficult to fit in all of the data you feel you need to publish to provide a full account of your research. Alternatively, you may find you have data that you should provide the reader but isn't necessarily key to the main storyline of your research. This is where the supplementary or appendix data comes in! Crucially, information should go to the supplementary if it resolves a deficiency in the manuscript. Information should be provided as an appendix if it is not essential to the manuscript's completeness. It can be difficult to figure out if you should include a supplement or an appendix, so take guidance from your supervisor.

Key Point: Researching the journal's requirements before writing up will save you a lot of time and frustration – especially with respect to figures and images!

SUPERVISORS AS A RESOURCE

Your supervisor will have published lots of academic manuscripts, so they will be a great help whilst you write up. Additionally, your group will be used to dealing with the type of information and data you have produced from your study, so they will probably have a lot of tips about making appropriate figures or graphs. Your group may even have access to special software to make this an easier process!

Asking for advice and help is a skill that students develop throughout their time at university, including their research project. Your supervisor will not be less impressed by you just because you asked for their advice – indeed, not asking for their guidance and then wasting time will probably not impress them!

Key Point: Don't be afraid to ask for guidance from your supervisor or other lab members.

WORKING IN GROUPS

Throughout your school life, you will have worked in teams and groups both in class and during extracurricular activities. Working in groups at university can be a different experience because:

- You may not know your teammates very well or at all!
- Your team members are all passionate about the course and subject
- Your team members are from different backgrounds and bring different life experiences to the group
- University assignments are more complicated than schoolwork

Working in groups can be a great academic experience as you will be exposed to a broad range of opinions and interpretations. You will also have the opportunity to explain your own unique perspective to others. In addition, it may be more efficient to share a large task between a team. Beyond the academic benefits, working in a group at university can help you develop communication, negotiation and teamwork skills that will be useful after university too. Most students underestimate how much employers value candidates that have evidence that they can work well in a team. Good teamwork is central to any successful company or organisation, and so developing these skills and demonstrating your ability will make you a much more attractive candidate when applying for jobs.

> **Key Point:** University group work can help you develop transferable skills that you will need after university!

HOW TO BE AN EFFECTIVE TEAM

It is always a good idea to start off group work by making sure everyone knows each other – this is best done by going around the group and saying your name (and sometimes, a cringey, funny fact about yourself!) Even if you feel comfortable in this group, you don't know how other group members feel and this activity can help settle the team in. It is a standard exercise many teams do in the industry and adopting this habit into your group practice only takes a couple of minutes.

Once your group has been orientated, it is important to make sure everyone knows what the group's purpose is. This step is usually not necessary when you're in a group to complete an assigned academic task, but it can be helpful to jot down the main question or task, the mark scheme or marks available, and the deadline to remind the group. It is also helpful to have a goal for your team to all work towards, whether that is full marks on your assignment or submitting your work to a conference. Make sure your goal is SMART (please see *How to Revise* chapter), and that your whole team agrees that it is a good goal to work towards!

When a new group has formed, it is important to create a few group values or rules. These can help to set the tone of the group, and can be used when dealing with tricky group dynamics or situations. Example values include:

- What's discussed in the meeting stays here, so any ideas are welcome
- This is a judgement free zone
- When disagreeing with an idea, that is all we are doing! We are not disagreeing with the creator or their beliefs

Group work requires trust between the team members – this means that individuals are able to ask for help, and share mistakes without being ostracised. Most students can find establishing trust in a group difficult in university group work settings because often, the students don't know each other well. Group values can help to establish a safe zone for those who may be feeling less comfortable or familiar with the group. Silly ice-breaking activities or even social activities like dinner or crazy golf can really help build trust, especially if the group is working on a long term project.

> Key Point: Effective teams are goal-orientated and trust each other!

GROUP DYNAMICS

There are several roles within a group dynamic, even if these roles are not formally recognised. These roles include the leader, supporter, executor, and the facilitator, and it is possible to occupy more than one role simultaneously or change roles during the task. Only you can decide what role(s) you will take on, and these may change depending on what your group or task looks like.

- The Leader   The leader of the group will make decisions that determine the direction of the group work. A good leader will listen to the opinions of the other team members, motivate the team, and make merit-based decisions. Although every group member can contribute to the tone of the group, the leader ultimately sets the tone. It's important to note that usually leaders are pre-determined, but occasionally a group member might develop into a group leader.

There are multiple leadership styles and a good skill is being able to identify the type of leadership your group needs. If your group is very vocal, you may be able to take a step back from the conversation to absorb all views then decide what to do. In other cases, you may have to take a more active approach in guiding conversations and assigning tasks to the group. You don't need to lead in one single way – a good leader is able to change leadership style as a team and task evolves.

If you are leading your group, you must remember that each team member is an independent adult, just like you! As a team leader, there is a power dynamic in your favour when you professionally interact with any other team member. As such, treating every member equally and with respect is crucial to maintain an open, productive relationship. Validating your team members' contributions can encourage others to offer their views and ideas. It also makes each team member feel valued and useful. Try to always acknowledge someone's contribution, even if you don't think it has added great value to the discussion! Phrases like 'that's an interesting viewpoint' or 'taking that into account, perhaps we should...' can be useful. The key thing to remember is to appreciate everyone's efforts and contributions without being patronising.

Remember, a leader should not take on every task and role in the team – you already have a role to lead! Some students find it difficult to allow their team members to do the work assigned to them and can stray into micro-management. This style of leadership is almost always counterproductive and disempowers your teammates from using their own skillset and initiative. It's natural to want to check on progress and this can be done in more polite and productive ways. If you are struggling with letting go of some micro-management tendencies, some students find a useful middle step to pre-schedule 'check up meetings' with your team, to monitor progress. This means that the whole team are aware of when they need to update you with their progress and prevents you from asking them at any other time!

Many students have a period during which they doubt their leadership skills and the decisions they've made as leader. Sometimes it's impossible to tell if you've made the right decision, but be confident that second guessing yourself is a natural response to leadership. In fact, self-reflecting on your performance makes you a better leader and demonstrates that you care! If your leadership responsibilities are too much, remember you have an entire team that can support you, so always reach out to them – their diverse perspectives can help you solve whatever problem you have.

- The Supporter

Sometimes, you will take a supporting role in the group. This essentially means that you aren't in a leadership role but take on any responsibility or task that will help the team achieve their goal. A supporter is a good team player, whose priority is the team and the team's goal. As supporters generally aren't immediately involved in making decisions, they can be well placed to offer impartial advice to the leader and team.

To be a good supporter, students must be open to taking whatever suitable tasks they are assigned by the team leader, but also know what tasks they are not suited to! Hopefully your team leader will recognise the team members' individual strengths and weaknesses, but don't be afraid to say you may be suited to a different task.

- The Organiser

Sometimes, a team member should take on the role as the organiser. The organiser is someone who keeps track of team tasks and deadlines, and ensure that the team is accountable for them. Some teams call this role a 'time keeper' but that title doesn't fully describe the role of the executor. In addition to checking in and seeing how team members are progressing with their tasks, an organiser will also see what support the team member will need to finish their task.

Sometimes, it can be helpful if the organiser is not the team leader, because it can involve chasing people for work! This is less frustrating to the team if they are all aware that the follow up they are receiving is from a peer who has been assigned this role. Additionally, an organiser will look at the details of a task to see if it is a reasonable amount of work to do in a set period time.

By doing this, they will also be familiar with the smaller requirements for certain tasks to be done, for example, they may identify an order that the tasks must be completed in or know the date the craft materials needed will be shipped by. The leader's perspective is generally of the whole project, rather than the minute details, which the organiser usually can see. The best organisers will empower their teammates and support them to complete their tasks. They take the administrative and organisational work away from the team members so they can focus on the task at hand.

- The Facilitator

A facilitator will ensure every member of the team has the opportunity and environment to thrive. They actively ensure or invite every team member to offer their opinions and views. A good group leader will also be a facilitator, but other group members can also play an important role in ensuring every voice is heard.

Being a facilitator can be difficult, however, because the role requires a level of maturity and professionalism, some students find it easier to adopt this role, as facilitating can be quite artificial and require you to actively disregard your own personal reactions to conversations. Facilitators can sometimes lead conversations, especially between two other groups members, as they can join as an 'external voice', preventing difficult conversations from becoming personal or awkward.

Key Point: Professionalism and mutual respect is central to all roles within a group.

COMMON PROBLEMS WITH GROUP WORK

It is common to have some problems when you're working in a team, even if you have a common goal and know what the task is. Most problems are due to poor communication or understanding, which can waste time and be very frustrating! Remember that communication is made up of two parts: the speaker and the listener. For complex tasks, you can check listener understanding by asking them to repeat what you said in their own words. You can also do this if you are the listener! That way, mistakes in communication can be identified early. If this strategy doesn't suit your team, then many students write up minutes of meetings and include action points or task lists. Action points should contain a small task to complete, the deadline, and who is responsible for the task. These documents can be sent around the group so they can refer back to them as a reminder of what was decided.

Occasionally you may experience some group members who don't do the tasks assigned to them or attend meetings. This problem is less common than what you may have experienced at school, as your team members will be adults who have chosen to study this course. As such, try to approach this team member with some compassion – there may be a very good reason for their absences. If the team member doesn't have a reason for their lack of participation, resist the urge to tell them off! Although this will make you feel better, telling your team member off will not make them work harder. Try revisiting your team values or goals to remind them of why they are there. It also could help to review the roles within the team and allocation of tasks.

> **Key Point:** Without clear communication, your group could waste time and get very frustrated!

DEBATE SKILLS

Some degree courses will contain academic debates, or you might get involved in your university's debating society! Many students find the first time they attend a debate to be very intimidating – there usually is a range of very confident and poised speakers that are passionately presenting their speeches. However, debating is a skill that anyone can learn and become a master of! Many of the best debaters started off as shy and under-confident students, who over time found that they really enjoyed debating. There are plenty of debate competitions across the UK and internationally that many university debate societies enter, so it can take you all over the world! Beyond debating as a fun extra-curricular activity, debating is a brilliant way to develop speaking, communication, and presentation skills so it can be viewed very favourably by future employers!

Debates that form part of your course are rarely graded, but can be a really useful learning tool to ensure you understand all sides of complex topics or issues. These debates can be great preparation for exam essay writing, as you have to form arguments quickly that are supported by evidence.

> **Key Point:** Debating is a great way to learn communication and speaking skills that can look very attractive to future employers!

STRUCTURE OF UK DEBATING

In the UK, most debating societies and competitions follow the structure of British Parliamentary debates (BP). In BP, there are two sides (also known as benches) called the Proposition and the Opposition. The Opposition must either support or oppose the motion that the Proposition proposes. Each bench is made up of 2 separate teams, each consisting of 2 speakers. This means there are 4 speakers per bench, totalling 8 speakers in the debate.

Once the teams are assembled, each bench is given the motion at the same time (either at the debate or emailed out before!) and 15 minutes of preparation time before the debate starts. The speeches last 7 minutes, and this time limit can be quite strict. A fairly unique element of the BP debating style is that the first and last minute of each speech is 'protected', which means the speaker can deliver the speech without any interruptions. The middle 5 minutes are vulnerable as the other bench can raise 'points of information', which are pointed and direct questions designed to throw off the speaker's fluency and arguments. If the other bench offers a 'point of information', the speaker must address this 'point of information' before returning to their speech. 'Points of information' are designed to derail the speaker's speech but in order for the bench to ask their 'point of information', the speaker must accept it. It is advised that speakers take at least one 'point of information' during their speech.

There are 4 speakers per bench and each have their own role to play:

1.	Opening Proposition 1st Speaker	This speech presents the Proposition's motion, which can be either for or against a topic. The speech will contain about 3 or 4 main arguments that the motion is built around. It must also define key words or concepts for the debate.
2.	Opening Opposition 1st Speaker	This speech rebuts the first presentation of the Proposition's case. It may present a counter – motion or the speech can systematically destroy the Proposition's motion.
3.	Opening Proposition 2nd Speaker	This second opening speech can rebut the Opposition's 1st speaker's case and rebuild any case that was rebutted by the Opposition. The speech may include new arguments supporting the Proposition's motion or build on previous arguments.

4. Opening Opposition 2nd Speaker

The last opening speech is made by the Opposition, who rebuts both speeches made by the Proposition and rebuilds the opposing case brought forward in the first Opposition argument.

5. Closing Proposition 1st Speaker

This speech rebuts the opening Opposition speeches and brings in new material, including arguments, analysis, and rebuttals.

6. Closing Opposition 1st Speaker

This speech rebuts the Proposition speeches and brings in new material, including arguments, analysis, and rebuttals.

7. Closing Proposition 2nd Speaker

Speakers are not allowed to introduce new material into this speech. It must summarise the debate, usually acknowledging the Opposition's arguments, and describes how the Proposition has overcome the Opposition's view.

8. Closing Opposition 2nd Speaker

Speakers are not allowed to introduce new material into this speech. It must summarise the debate, usually acknowledging the Proposition's arguments, and describes how the Proposition has overcome the Proposition's view.

Key Point: Debates in the UK are formal events that follow a very traditional structure. To get the most out of your experience, make sure you're familiar with the structure before going to a debate!

COMMON QUESTIONS ABOUT DEBATING

Learning how to debate can be a steep learning curve but once you get the hang of the debate structure and how to approach debating, it can be much more enjoyable! This section will cover some of the common questions and guidance students need when starting debating:

> *'I didn't go to a private school and have never debated before. I don't think this is the activity for people like me'*
>
> It should be acknowledged that debating started out as an activity that attracted predominantly male identifying people from privileged backgrounds. Today at university level, debating is a diverse activity, with active attempts to encourage people from all backgrounds to give it a go. There will be a mix of experienced and novice debaters in every society, but the activity has moved on from its elitist history.

> *'When I try to make up rebuttals or arguments, I don't sound clever enough'*
>
> When students first try debating, they can feel a self-inflicted pressure to sound super intelligent and impressive. When you deliver your first speech, remember to speak from your heart and be natural – the arguments that you deliver most easily are often the most convincing!

'I really struggle with improvising arguments during debates'

If you're struggling to find arguments for a motion, take your time to think about what the motion really means. Don't panic and take your time:

- Think about the surrounding context of the motion – are there any real-life relevant examples that you can think of?
- Any immediate issues that the motion doesn't address, or creates? Does the motion go far enough to address what it means to (this is a really common issue with motions, so can be a great place to start thinking of rebuttals!)
- Think of how the other bench might say, so you can anticipate their rebuttal by building up a case against their future objections!

'I like thinking up arguments and writing speeches, but talking in front of people is my worst nightmare'

Most students that lack confidence speaking in public or in front of larger groups of people believe that they alone face this problem. There are hundreds of students involved in debating who find public speaking frightening but use several strategies to overcome their fear and feel confident when standing up and delivering a speech. Many students focus on a point in the room, like a clock on the wall, whilst delivering their speech so they can ignore all of the people and other debaters. This can detract from your delivery but this drawback can be minimised by choreographing your body language and hand gestures to engage the audience. Other students find practising their speaking in front of people whose opinions they really respect can be the best way to alleviate their fears. In essence, this strategy plays on the greater anxiety caused by speaking in front of a person you respect versus a group of strangers. Lastly, some students find that dressing in a 'power outfit' or clothes they wouldn't normally wear, enables them to assume enough confidence to speak in front of a crowd. Some of these strategies may sound silly or ineffective at first glance, but try them out and see if they make you feel empowered and ready to take the stage!

CRITICAL THINKING

An essential skill to develop and demonstrate at university is critical thinking. Critical thinking assesses the validity and strength of evidence presented, a topic we have touched on with the levels of evidence section in the Understanding Research Papers chapter. Almost all academic publications go through a process called peer review, in which several independent experts from that field will evaluate the research and suggest improvements. Some publications may go through several revisions before the panel is satisfied with the output. Peer review is a great mechanism to guarantee a set standard within a journal, however, each journal will have its own peer review guidelines and each peer reviewer is a human being who can make mistakes! As such, although most research published in academic journals is reliable and truthfully reported, each study has potential bias and limitations.

Lots of students believe that critical thinking can only be negative and involve evaluating the weaknesses of research, but in fact critical thinking involves noting the limitations and appreciating the strengths of evidence. This chapter will guide you through the foundations of critical thinking, so you can apply this skill to any source or evidence.

> **Key Point:** Critical thinking involves evaluating the reliability of evidence and information.

WHEN TO USE CRITICAL THINKING

During university, critical thinking should be used whenever students read original research or use sources as evidence in their work. As such, you should apply critical thinking when encountering information in seminars or lectures and also in your written work. Critical thinking is also a transferable skill that you can use when encountering any piece of information or news beyond university. The evaluative skills you will develop through critical thinking at university are also highly valued in industry and by future employers.

Critical thinking can help students to:

- Identify the most relevant and strong evidence
- Assess the validity of the study
- Assess the usefulness of evidence
- Recognise any bias in the resource
- Discard any weak evidence
- Reach evidence-based conclusions

> **Key Point:** Critical thinking is a highly transferable skill that is valued by all types of future employers.

HOW TO CRITICALLY EVALUATE INFORMATION

Many students struggle at university when they are instructed to critically evaluate information because they are rarely given a framework to approach critical thinking. Some universities offer workshops to develop these skills and these can be a very useful resource, but you may have work assignments before these workshops are available. This section will describe a basic framework for you to help you approach critical evaluation of any source or information. There isn't a precise checklist that you must work through to 'correctly' critically evaluate information, instead, you can use this framework to guide your approach and perspective when reading sources and information.

1. Publication information	Take a step back from the information you are assessing and see where it has come from. If you're looking at a primary research paper, the research project may be the first recording of this information, or there may be a citation indicating where the original evidence and information can be found. To be thorough, you may consider reading any papers that are cited and linked to your information and applying critical thinking to those too.

If the information is published in an academic journal, have a look at which journal it is from. If the paper is from a well-known, internationally leading journal, you can be more reassured of the providence of information than if it is sourced form a smaller, independent journal. Many students incorrectly believe that if information comes from an academic journal, then it is trustworthy and good quality information. Remember that even information from academic journals should be critically analysed!

If the information is not from an academic journal, you should consider any political or industry ties that the publisher may have and any other potential causes of bias.

2. Overall Study Design

If your information source is from any type of research, look at the overall methodology of the study and identify any intrinsic limitations in the approach. For example, if your information has come from a literature search, see how many databases, the timespan, and type of publications included. If the source is a primary research article, have a general look at the type of study and consider the level of evidence this study (see the Understanding Research Papers chapter)

3. Population

If your information is derived from population-based research, have a look at the population characteristics which are usually presented in a table quite early on in the results section. Is this population similar to the population the information is being applied to? If not, then your information probably isn't relevant or even valid for what it's being used for!

If your information is not from research, you should still evaluate the population the information was formed from. Similarly, to any research population, if the group used to form the information is not similar to the group the information is being applied to, then it's probably not being used correctly.

4. Research Sources only: Research Question

The next step is to read the research question(s) and aims, and see if the paper has actually answered the questions posed! Look at the question(s) posed and see if the research addresses these aims. Consider if there may have been alternate experiments or research that could answer the question with stronger evidence. Many students forget this step, but some projects compromise study design and strength of evidence produced with other factors such as economic cost and time.

5. Results

If your information is based off of data, use the data provided, figures and graphs, and any relevant information you can request from the original author, to evaluate if the conclusions made are supported by the raw data. Many students find this to be the trickiest step of critical thinking, as it requires some data interpretation. If you are struggling, a good place to start is using the visual representations of data, for example, the graphs and tables. See if you can identify a trend or correlative relationship between the two factors. Then, apply this correlation to the conclusion and see if the two agree!

6. Author information and conflicts of interests

The last step is to check for any bias introduced by the authors or investigators themselves. At the end of research papers and books, there will always be a 'declaration of interests', where the authors have to submit any funding or sponsorship they receive from related companies or institutions. You should be aware that authors receiving money may influence the way the study has been conducted to skew the results in favour of their sponsor's interests. This is rare, but you must always evaluate for this possibility!

If you are using a quotation, then you must consider the context in which the person said these words. For example, a quote from the US Secretary of Defence during the Cold War will be influenced by multiple factors including the public opinion, the government's agenda, and Russia's perceived stance and strength at the time.

The framework above is a basic guide that you can use to start critically analysing your sources and information. Although it seems like there are a lot of steps to go through and things to consider for each piece of information you will come across, with more practice you will be able to critically appraise information very quickly! The framework above is a great structure to help you approach thinking critically about any source of information.

THEORY OF KNOWLEDGE

Most university students go to university hoping to increase their knowledge and awareness of their course subject. But how can we accept things as knowledge? How do we 'know' knowledge? What even is knowledge?!

The theory of knowledge attempts to answer these questions, but the nature of knowledge has been a contentious concept over hundreds of years! This chapter will outline the main proposal and thoughts on this philosophical topic. As such, this chapter may not directly help you answer a question you face at university, unlike the other chapters in this book, however, it offers you the chance to approach knowledge from a different perspective.

Overall, the Theory of Knowledge attempts to organise an approach to knowledge, including defining what knowledge is, the ways to know knowledge, and lastly, organising knowledge content into categories.

> **Key Point:** The Theory of Knowledge is an area of thinking and philosophy that tries to make sense of what knowledge actually is and how we understand knowledge.

HISTORICAL FOUNDATIONS OF THE THEORY OF KNOWLEDGE

The Theory of Knowledge attempts to address conceptual questions like 'what is knowledge?'. It is proposed that the theory of knowledge was first debated by the Ancient Greeks, and their theories still pervade the theory of knowledge today! The main contributors included philosophers Aristotle, Plato, Socrates, and Democritus, amongst others. These philosophers tried to define knowledge and reason how we accept something as knowledge:

- Plato defined four stages of knowledge development: imagining, belief, thinking, and perfect intelligence. He thought that knowledge must be both real and infallible (never failing) to be true knowledge. Any knowledge that cannot prove that it is real and infallible, is a false belief and therefore, cannot be true belief.

- Socrates stated that knowledge is the same as virtue. Here, Socrates sees a virtue as goodness or a concept of goodness. Knowledge, therefore, is something that has universal appeal or acceptance by people that 'does good for', or supports, existing concepts.
- Democritus' interpretation of knowledge and thought brings in the concepts of perception. Democritus believed that thought was due to images outside of the body influencing the body's state. As such, thought was defined as changes in the body. This school of thought touches on another philosophical problem about perception and the world. This problem debates the issue that our perceptions of the world provides our knowledge but this perception isn't direct contact with the 'nature of things' (with the real world itself), and so it can lead to false belief or incorrect 'knowledge'.
- Lastly, Aristotle's view of knowledge was similar to Plato's. Aristotle believed that knowledge is of what is real and this realness must be proven to be true.

Key Point: Overall, these theories suggest that knowledge is an overlap of truth and belief.

KNOWLEDGE, FACTS, AND TRUTH

In light of the Theory of Knowledge, it can be difficult to appreciate the reasons why we conduct research and what meaning the results have. It's important to consider that research data is ultimately an estimation and demonstration of the most likely result. Indeed, the definition of statistical significance is often '$p = < 0.5$'. which really means that the likelihood of these results being due to chance is 5%. So, 1 in 20 times this result will happen because of random chance. As such, scientific proof is a demonstration that the result is the most possible event. Most knowledge and well-known accepted facts are made from an entire base of research, so the probability of the event or fact being correct, is very close to absolutely proven, however, there is not 100% probability or proof of any research conclusion!

Another dilemma raised by the Theory of Knowledge touches on perception and reality. Arguably, perception is reality because it's your interpretation of the world and what you experience. Your perception and experiences shape who you are and make you unique! No person will experience the exact same thing, and so reality for each person is slightly different.

A good example of this is colour, as no one sees colour the exactly the same way as another person. However, two people looking at a coloured piece of paper can agree that there is a coloured piece of paper, but may not agree on all of the details about what type of colour it is! At a university you will meet a vast range of people and their perceptions may be very different from yours. You may not agree with their view, and you don't have to! But what you must always appreciate is that there is a person behind this view, and whilst you may not respect their points, you must respect the person. This is the basis of academic discussion (please see the Structuring Academic Discussion chapter).

THE PROCESS OF ACQUIRING KNOWLEDGE

There are so many strategies we use to learn things but why do they work? How do we acquire new knowledge? The Theory of Knowledge proposes 4 ways through which we can acquire knowledge:

- Perception: You can acquire new knowledge by its effect on you and knowledge is therefore, your interpretation of experiences

- Emotion: You can acquire new knowledge through how it makes you feel, for example, you may have a gut feeling that something is wrong.

- Language: Other people can convey this knowledge to you, either via written text or by speaking

- Reason: You can acquire new knowledge through logical deduction

Similar to the philosophical problem that perception is an interpretation and experience of the world rather than a direct interaction, all of these ways to acquire knowledge is indirect. Language provides knowledge in a 'second - hand' manner. Reason is 'second-hand' because your logical interpretations will be influenced they way you think, which is formed by everything that you have experienced before! Emotion and perception are also personalised responses to an external stimulus. As such, some people argue that facts don't exist, rather are pieces of knowledge that just like Socrates said, are 'virtues' that are universally accepted. It is important to note that because each of these methods of acquiring knowledge are 'second-hand', they all offer the opportunity for false knowledge or beliefs to be acquired. For example, the language process of acquiring knowledge can introduce false knowledge through reading fake news or information from an unreliable source.

> **Key Point:** There are four 'ways of knowing' knowledge. These processes each have an opportunity for incorrect knowledge to be acquired.

AREAS OF KNOWLEDGE

The Theory of Knowledge splits up knowledge into broad areas and states that we categorise knowledge into these areas in order to understand them. Typically, the areas include:

- The Arts
- History
- The Human Sciences
- Mathematics
- The Natural Sciences

But some other sources also include areas like ethics, religious knowledge systems and indigenous knowledge systems.

RECEIVING GRADES AND EXAMINATION RESULTS

As part of your university course, you will submit work and sit examinations that will be used to assess you as a student. Sometimes, the grades you receive will not be as you expect – whether they are higher or lower than what you wanted, in either case you will often want to know why. Sometimes, you can request feedback from the person who set the work, or test, and reflecting on this feedback can be extremely useful. With end-of-year tests and university-wide examinations, this is less likely, and your results should instead be taken as a broad indication of how well you have absorbed the content of the course.

Additionally, at the end of your course, you will receive a degree class or classification, which is the overall mark that you have earned for your university degree. At school, you may have been graded on a scale from A* - U, or 1 – 10. At UK universities, degrees can be awarded in several categories:

- First class

  This can be awarded to students who have achieved 70% or above in their overall examined marks.

- Second class

  There are two categories in this degree class. The first category is an upper second-class degree, which is awarded to students that achieve 60% or more, all the way up to 70% (non – inclusive). This is also known as a two-one, written as 2:1.

  A lower second – class degree is awarded to students who achieve 50 – 60% in their exams and is also called a 2:2 (a two- two). Although this is still a second-class degree, employers consider a lower second – class degree less attractive than an 2:1.

- Third class honours

  Students who score between 40 and 50% gain a third-class degree. In most universities, this is the lowest class of degree possible.

WAITING FOR EXAMINATION RESULTS

Many university students find it really difficult to discover and process what they earned in exams or an important assignment. There can be a lot of reasons for this:

- The student worked extremely hard and is worried that their grade doesn't reflect their effort
- The grade or exam has a large impact on their overall degree class
- The student feels that the grade is a true appraisal of their intelligence and self-worth
- The exam didn't go very well at the time and so the grade won't reflect their ability
- It is the first graded work the student has completed at university, and the student doesn't know where they lie within their class or on a university marking scale

As you can see, whether you feel like an exam or assignment went well or badly, being nervous for results day is completely valid and very common amongst students. Being nervous is a sign that you care about your results, which isn't a bad reason for your feelings!

Most universities will take at least a few weeks to mark all of the examined work, whether this is a dissertation or an exam paper. Some courses will only release marks at the end of the academic year, so you can wait up to 10 months to find out your grades. For some students, they experience peaks of grade related anxiety after they have completed their exams which then fades away until a few days before results are due out. Other students find they have a low level of stress throughout the waiting period or just stress suddenly comes on the night before.

With all kinds of stress, it is valuable to bear in mind that, while your exam results and grades are very important, they do not have any impact on your value as a person, or your strength of character. If your grades are below what you expected, it is very normal to feel disappointed, sad, or anxious – but the impact that a bad grade will have on your life in the years to come may be negligible.

Whatever pattern of stress you may experience, exam and grade related anxiety should not take over your life or dominate your mind. It is really important to be self-aware of your feelings and mindset. That way you can seek support from friends, family, and healthcare professionals to help you manage the stressful period. If you are very worried or stressed, it can be really difficult to self-reflect and realise that you may need some support. If you're not sure how you are managing, that's probably a sign that you may need a little support, and often university counselling services will provide short term counselling sessions or workshops to help students navigate through exam related stress. Alternatively, you can always seek support from your local healthcare providers or educational adviser.

If you need to talk to someone and don't know where to turn to, experiencing acute distress, or suddenly feel like you are not managing your stress levels, you can always call to chat to an adviser or counsellor at your university, or at a range of other options, including but not limited to:

- Samaritans, a charity open every day and every hour of the year — 116 123
- NHS (urgent medical advice) — 111
- NHS (urgent medical help) — 999 or visit your local Accident and Emergency Department

PREPARING FOR POSTGRADUATE LIFE

It is never too early to start thinking about postgraduate life, but you should view this chapter in different ways depending on how far you are in to your university course. If you are more than 2 years from graduating, read this chapter to gain an awareness and understanding of the postgraduate processes you will have to go through to gain employment, further study, or an internship. If you are around 2 years or less from your graduation, you should use this chapter to help you make some headway on applications, CV writing, and references. In your last year of university, no matter where you are, what you're studying or where you want to go after university, you will be exceptionally time poor. It is best to start early so you can dedicate the time your future deserves to any application or plans you need to make. Additionally, some international scholarships have deadlines that are out of sync with the UK academic year, so you may need to apply for them 2 academic years before you graduate.

Your future is so exciting – you have so many opportunities and chances to take! However, all students find the end of their university course stressful. Exams, applications, and interviews combined can be really tough to tackle. Added to this is an ever-present feeling of uncertainty about the future. Take it one step at a time and remember you are not alone! There are plenty of university support services, like the university counselling service, your academic advisers or supervisors, and professors, who will be happy to give you a helping hand through this period of your life. Family and friends who care about you may have opinions about what you should do too. These can be helpful but students can receive some unwelcome advice or even pressure sometimes! To prevent this, it can help to remind them at the start of this process, that your future is ultimately up to you, but their caring advice is welcome. This conversation can prevent a lot of emotional arguments. Setting this boundary later, when emotions and tensions can be high on both sides of the conversation is much less helpful. It can also be helpful to remind yourself that everyone giving you their opinions and advice is doing so because they care about you – write this on a notecard and stick it on your toothbrush!

> **Key Point:** Planning for the future can be scary, but remember that everyone around you cares and wants the best for you!

POSTGRADUATE LIFE OPTIONS

Every student is different and the path that you will take is unique to your friends. It is important to take some time to reflect on what you want to accomplish after you leave university. Remember, your first job or experience after university is most likely not going to be what you specifically end up doing for the rest of your life, even if you study a vocational course like Medicine, so don't put too much pressure on yourself to choose your life direction. Just figure out what you want to do right now and form a SMART goal (please see How to Revise Chapter). Note, your friends and family might influence your thinking or even add pressure for you to go in a certain direction, but make sure you choose what you want.

Instead of thinking about specific career pathways or further education, it may help you to reframe the question. Ask yourself: 'what are my priorities?' Your main priority might narrow down your options and help you realise what opportunities you need to take to get you to your goal. For example, if you crave financial stability, you may choose to look at careers that will offer this and see what postgraduate education is helpful (or even required) to pursue this area.

After reflecting on your priorities, if you still have no idea what you want to do, make an appointment with your university careers advice service. Consulting a professional may not give you an exact answer, but they will help structure your thinking! Students often find it more helpful to use this service after they have had some time to think about their options, but you can access this support at any point in your postgraduate planning journey. These services can also be helpful if you know what you want to pursue as they have supported hundreds of applicants before you, they will have some tips and tricks!

> **Key Point:** Deciding what to do and apply for after university can be tricky. Your university careers service is a resource for you to use and get the support you need!

CVS

Very few postgraduate opportunities will not require you to submit a curriculum vitae (CV). Lots of students have a rough draft of a CV already, but don't worry if you haven't written one. A CV is a formal document that has all relevant information about you, including:

- Brief contact details

- Educational background and achievements

- Awards and prizes

- Career aspirations

- Published works – academic or literature

- Conference presentations (poster or oral)

- Work history

- Contact details for references

You may be surprised to hear that you should have one CV (which some students fondly call 'the mega CV') that has every achievement and job you have ever had on. It is really easy to lose or forget about things you have done or achieved, so having a mega CV as a depository for your achievements can be very helpful. This mega CV can then be adapted for each application you make. To tailor your CV to an application, research the job and make sure key buzz words about the job are addressed in your CV, for example, teamwork or innovation.

CVs have a generally accepted format and structure. Generally, CVs should not exceed 2 sides of A4 and must be written in a clear and professional font such as Arial or Times New Roman. Your CVs layout plays a really important role in structuring the information and presenting you as a good candidate for whatever you are applying for. You should use headings, spaces, and bullet points to highlight information. On the next page we have provided a basic template to help you get started.

Many students don't realise that they should get feedback on their CV – it is like any other part of an application! Although you may not have encountered asking for CV feedback, it is a completely normal thing to do, so ask your education advisers, the university careers service, your friends, and any industry contacts to take a look. Much of postgraduate life is advocating for yourself, so this is a perfect opportunity to practise!

Key Point: CVs should be tailored to each application. This can take a lot of time but it is worth it in the end!

Write your full first and second name here
On the next line, write your address
Insert your email address; and your phone number here

Before you start listing your achievements, you should write a very short biography for yourself. Include who you are (professionally), for example 'I am a recently graduate in...' and where your career or academic interests lies. This biography should be about 3 or 4 lines long

Education

Your degree type (BSc, BA), Your University or College   *Year*
Write any exam achievements you may have here

Insert any other degrees in the lines below.   *Year*

Relevant Experience

Job Title. *Brief information about the job you did and what skills you demonstrated here.* *Start and end year*

This job description may be up to three lines long, but don't just write for the sake of writing - be concise!
Job Title. *Brief information about the job you did and what skills you demonstrated here.* *Start and end year*

Job Title. *Brief information about the job you did and what skills you demonstrated here.* *Start and end year*

Job Title. *Brief information about the job you did and what skills you demonstrated here.* *Start and end year*

Awards

Award Title. *Brief description of the award, in particular how competitive it was or why it as awarded. Also include the awarding body.* *Year*

Publications and Research

Title. Journal. *Brief description of the work you conducted. You can leave out this section if you are not applying for an academic job or studentship.*
Year

References

Either write your two references here and indicate if they are academic or professional references, or you can write 'references upon asking', which can be useful if you haven't confirmed your references at the time of applying!

REFERENCES

For job and academic applications, you will need to provide references alongside your application. A lot of thought should go into choosing your referees (the people who write your reference). You may even choose to adapt who you choose as your referees depending on the application type.

Any person that you have worked for or been supervised by may write a reference for you. This includes your education adviser, project supervisors, and head of faculty. Generally, it is accepted to use references from people within the last two years of your university career. You should be aware that referees may refuse to write you a reference if they believe they aren't in a position to truly attest to your skills or work in that particular area. Additionally, you should never ask a friend or family to write a reference for you. After you have decided who to ask for a reference, you need to politely see if they are able to provide one! If you see them in person, ask them verbally and follow up with the necessary details by email – it is harder for them to say no if you ask in person! In your email, you should repeat (or ask for the first time) your request. You should also provide them with all the details they need to submit your reference – it will annoy your referee if they need to chase you up for more details, so make it easy for them to help you out! You must remember to email them with: the person they need to write to, the contact details, the job specification, and the deadline for the reference.

It is vital that you give your referees enough time to write your reference. It is common practise to ask referees approximately 4 weeks before the reference deadline. Occasionally, students discover a brilliant opportunity very close to the application deadline. If this is the case, you can still ask your references but be very polite and acknowledge the tight turn-around.

There are three different types of references, character, professional, and academic. The character reference will attest to who you are, placing your application in context with your extracurricular or personal achievements.

Your educational supervisor is a great person to give you a character reference, or if you have worked or volunteered during your degree, your manager could also provide this. A character reference is the most personal type of reference, as it is commenting on your character so it is really telling to future employers or admissions tutors if the referee doesn't really advocate for the student. As such, make sure you pick someone who knows you well and is invested in your future too!

A professional reference is written by your recent or current employer. As a university leaver, they are often optional to include (for example, you may be asked to provide 1 academic and 1 academic or professional reference). This is because not all students will have been employed during their course, so it would be unfair for them to need to supply one. As such, if you can supply a professional reference, it can be a tricky decision to decide if you should provide two strong academic references or an academic and professional reference. This decision is centred around making sure you submit the strongest references. You will probably not be able to see the references that will be submitted so to judge the strength of the reference you will have to guess based on your relationship with your referee and their experience in writing references. You should also factor in your referee's job title – if you have worked closely with a significant department or group head, then their name on your reference will be impressive in your application. Factoring in job titles and prestige into this decision can complicate it further – sometimes you may have a weaker reference from a prestigious source versus an exceptional reference from a lesser known professional. Unfortunately, only you can answer that in the context of the rest of your application, but remember to seek advice from other sources too! Returning to the original question of submitting two academic or an academic and professional reference, you should consider the following two things:

1. What does the second academic reference add to your application that the first (your strongest reference) doesn't?
2. What does your professional reference add to your application? Can you demonstrate your professional and transferable skills elsewhere in your application?

Sometimes there is no objective way to decide what references to include in your application. Make sure you ask advice from other people to help add different perspectives. At the end of the day, you may just need to make a decision and be at peace with that – a skill that takes a long time to develop in itself!

Lastly, your academic references can be written by any of your academic supervisors. Generally, anyone who is post-doctorate is an acceptable reference to academic and industrial institutions. If you are applying for prestigious scholarships, you may want to ask your group leader or head of division, but don't feel pressured to choose prestige over reference quality (please see the discussion in the professional reference paragraph above).

> **Key Point:** Once you decide who to ask to be your referee, references are the easiest part of the application!

RESEARCH PROPOSALS

If you are applying for a research – based degree, you will be asked to submit a research proposal with your application. A research proposal is a detailed outline of what research you would carry out if you were admitted to degree programme. You may also be asked to submit a research proposal after you have gained entry to a course and for funding applications, so this skill is vital if you want to succeed in academia! When applying for courses, universities generally state that they use the proposal to match you with a suitable supervisor, however in reality, you should have already found and chosen your supervisor and worked backwards from there! To do this, go onto the institution's website and have a look at the existing research groups. You should contact group leaders who are focusing on areas that interest you, and discuss potential projects. This can be quite daunting, but you need to advocate for yourself and your future! The research proposal is an important element of your application and so you should take a lot of time to write it. Make sure you ask your current supervisors, advisers, friends, and contacts to read through and offer feedback!

A research proposal should:

- Describe your proposed project
- Explain the significance of your proposed work in the context of the wider field
- Demonstrate that the research is original and innovative
- Explain why you are the right person to carry out this research

The application might request you write your research proposal in a particular structure, but generally you should include:

- Title

  Some students struggle writing a slick and descriptive title for their proposal, however, if you already have a good idea of your proposal, then writing the title first can focus your work further – it's up to you!

- Objectives

  You should write your objectives directly and in bullet point form. This will add clarity to your writing and ensure the admissions panel understands what you propose to do.

- Literature review

  Most students struggle when writing the justification, because it is essentially the argument for why your project is important and original. A good place to start is by thinking of this section as the introduction to your final research manuscript from this project. By writing an introduction, you will produce a slick background to the project and the 'problem' (please see the Publication and Academic Writing section) your research will address.

- A brief justification of your proposed research project, also known as the 'impact section'

    This section will require you to place your research in a broader context, both within the area of your study but perhaps also beyond. Some research will contribute to national policies, some will challenge popular beliefs, and others will create a platform for subsequent research. Think about the impact your research may have within your subject and in the context of research, and then also describe the wider implications beyond academia.

- Outline of methods

    Students usually find this section easiest to write. Similarly to writing a methods section for publications, you should clearly state what you will do with as much detail as possible (see Publication chapter for more details).

- Confidentiality and ethics

    This section is usually a form or pre-written document for you to fill in that also has a space for you to write any measures you will take to protect the confidentiality of any participants. You will also need to declare any ethics you will need to apply for and what councils will be consulted. If you get stuck on this section, your current research supervisor or education adviser will be able to help you with this!

- References

    Insert references for any citations you have made in your proposal. Please see the guidance in the Fundamentals of Referencing Chapter for more information.

- Proposed research schedule

  You should provide a rough timeline of your research project. This should be realistic, so make sure you give yourself enough time to accomplish each task!

- Budget or funding (if applicable)

  If funding is provided by the programme, you may need to provide a rough budget proposal. This will require a lot of research because researchers on the admissions panel will be familiar with the costs.

  If your programme doesn't come with funding, you may need to state a few places where you may apply for research funding. This will also require some research but is fairly simple to do!

Key Point: Research proposals are a crucial piece of your application. Make sure you take time and get a lot of feedback from your current

---

APPLICATION TESTS

For both jobs and further study, you may be required to sit extra exams or tests. These test scores are often used to shortlist candidates for interviews, sometimes even before recruiters have read your application. As such, it is crucial you score well! For tests you may have to complete for jobs, they are usually run at a test centre or even at the company office. Make sure you're wearing professional clothing, are polite to everyone there and just like an interview, don't let them see your nerves (always make a good impression!) Tests for postgraduate study are usually held at a generic test centre where other tests like the UK driving theory tests are run.

For academic applications, there are over 100 tests available, so make sure you have correctly researched which test your course requires. Both job and further study tests usually ask non-verbal, abstract, or verbal reasoning questions. You can use practise books to revise exam technique, which can radically improve your marks. It is crucial that you use the right resources for your test, so look on the test website to see what books they recommend. There are plenty of fake revision books from less reputable sources that are looking to profit from your anxiety. If the test website doesn't recommend any resources, look for more generic question books from reputable authors and publishers.

> **Key Point:** Application tests can really help your application or act as a barrier to interviews. Make sure you prepare for the test correctly – work hard and work smart!

DEALING WITH REJECTION

All students dread receiving rejections. It can be really disappointing to be rejected, especially if you spent a long time on the application or you got really far in the recruitment process. It may even be your first time receiving a rejection. Students very rarely get the first jobs they apply for, as you refine your application and interview techniques as you apply for more jobs. If you are devasted by a rejection, that's ok – it's completely natural to be sad if you really wanted it. Give yourself a set amount of time, this might be a few hours or days, to wallow and feel disappointed in the result. After your set time is up, be strict with yourself and stop wallowing! Now is the time to distract yourself with other work, activities, family time, and fun stuff! When you can face looking at your applications again, it may be worthwhile to email the recruiter to ask for feedback on your application to improve it for the next cycle.

If you have received multiple rejections, try to seek some advice on how to improve your application as a whole – you may be missing a small but crucial element in your statements or CV which is easy to fix. It can be really hard to keep positive when you have received multiple rejections and made multiple applications for jobs. Make sure you allocate time to relax and step away from job applications. If you find you are struggling to cope with your situation, seek support from your university counselling service, careers service, education supervisor, or healthcare provider.

> **Key Point:** Receiving rejections can be hard so take time and look after yourself! You won't produce more quality job applications when you're in the wrong mindset.

ACADEMIC SKILLS CHECKLIST

By the end of university, you should be able to:

- Take good quality notes from any teaching or meeting session

- Use active listening skills to communicate with your peers and colleagues

- Take part in and moderate academic discussions

- Revise course content effectively

- Demonstrate good organisational skills and time management

- Use library resources confidently

- Conduct original research

- Find evidence and sources through academic and literature searches

- Appropriately use and evaluate evidence in your academic work

- Apply critical thinking to your academic work

- Confidently write in an academic and formal style

- Know how to submit your work to conferences and academic journals

- Work effectively in a team

- Feel empowered to tackle the next steps in your academic journey or career!

This book (and the list above!) has covered every academic skill that you will need over the course of your university degree. Now we have reached the end of the guide, you may feel slightly overwhelmed with the new skills you will acquire and develop over the next few years. Try to remember that every student will be learning these skills as they study too, so you are in the same boat as all of your peers! This book will familiarise you with all of the skills and experiences you will encounter at university, but remember, no student comes to university completely prepared or skilled to tackle a university education! Be patient with yourself and your personal development, and you will succeed!

FUN EXPERIENCES TO PREPARE YOU FOR ACADEMIA

Before you start university, you may warm up their brain and learn about UK university culture. This can be a really fun time and also can be quite reassuring, whilst you wait for your term to begin.

MUSEUMS

Before and during university, museums are a great day out! In major cities there will be larger museums, like the Museum of Natural History (London), the Science Museum (London), and the Discovery Museum (Newcastle). Usually entry is either free for students or children and quite reasonable for those who don't qualify as concessions. In the UK, museums are often in ancient buildings or purpose-built modern spaces, so their architecture is quite stunning, in addition to the displays! In addition to the larger and more famous museums, the UK will also have at least one museum dedicated to the subject you are studying – you may have to use a search engine to find it but it'll be a short train or car ride away!

Museums are a great place to walk around at your own pace and absorb information. In addition, it's fascinating to see collections of objects and art that all have significance and are evidence for our knowledge today. Most museums will have a restaurant and gardens too, so it can be a lovely way to spend the day out! Lots of students realise that museum visits can help and advance their learning during university, so visiting a few before you begin can give you a little advantage in class!

ART GALLERIES

Although art can be displayed in museums, art galleries are dedicated spaces that house only artwork. Whatever your course is, art is a brilliant way to introduce you to new perspectives and ways of thinking – art is even relevant to those studying Physics, Medicine, and Maths!

With each piece of work, you will find a small piece of information on a panel nearby which explains the significance and the artist's intentions when producing this work. This will help explain the work and make you see it through the artist's eyes. The art may even represent an experience or historic event, which you can learn about through the artist's perspective. After being encouraged to visit art galleries, many students approaching university have reported that the visits helped prepare them both academically and socially for the transition. Specifically, the galleries widened the student's awareness of different types of people and the range of what humans can experience.

There are small and big art galleries all over the UK, usually in larger towns and cities. Smaller galleries tend to display art from a few artists whereas some UK galleries contain works from hundreds of artists. Just like when you visit a museum, it can pay off to research the place you want to visit first. If you're not familiar with art galleries, visiting a larger display can be a good place to start, as you will be exposed to multiple artists and can get a feel for what art you personally prefer too! Art galleries can be free to enter but some charge – usually it is cheaper to book online ahead of the day! Remember to bring your student card with you for concession prices!

STATIONERY STORES

For most school leavers, preparing for university will also include acquiring household items for them to use, like saucepans and cutlery! Most students forget that they will need things like pens, paper, and notebooks too! A fun activity for you to in preparation for your academic life at university is visiting a stationery shop for your stationery needs. There are plenty of independent shops in the UK that are dedicated to stationery as well as a few well – known chain brands. Make sure you remember to get:

- A notebook
- Files for loose pages of notes
- Pens
- Pencil, pencil sharpener and rubber
- Any specific paper if you are an art or architecture student
- Post stick notes

There are some great designs for every type of student and you will be amazed at the range available! Take your friends and go kit yourselves out for university!

BOOKS AND MAGAZINES

There are quite a range of knowledge based easy-reading books available at mainstream bookstores. Some are autobiographies, comedic retellings of experiences in certain jobs, and others are slightly more academic works discussing historic events or scientific concepts. These books can be a great way to reintroduce academic work and get you thinking about concepts whilst relaxing over the summer! This activity isn't just about reading the books – instead, visit your local bookstore and take your time looking at the different books on offer. You may be able to get a student discount at some retailers and independent shops too!

There are also some magazines that are hybrids of popular magazines and academic journals. Any larger bookshop will carry a range of magazines so if reading a book is a bit more work than you want to do during your break before university (and that's a very valid feeling to have!), you can always have a flick through some magazines!

The books and magazines don't have to be specifically focussed on your subject – you can use this as an opportunity to do some wider reading, which will always improve and add to your perspective when encountering your course content! Don't feel any pressure to read lots of books and heaving journals – only do it if it's something that appeals to you! It's a fun activity and absolutely not expected of students before university!

PODCASTS, TALKS AND DOCUMENTARIES

Some students don't find reading accessible or enjoyable to do in their spare time. If you didn't identify at all with the books and magazines section above, you could alternatively explore podcasts, talks and documentaries online! There are plenty of free streaming services and institutions that publish their talks online for free, so look up a topic or subject area you are interested in, and go from there! Live academic talks also take place in all major cities and university towns and can be a great way to spend an evening. You can also meet current university students there and potentially some professors in the field! These talks are often free and talk schedules can be found online!

It can often take a little more effort to locate talks, podcasts, or documentaries that you are interested in rather than just heading to your local bookstore, they can be great fun and a brilliant way to warm up for university!

AFTERWORD

Your time at university will provide you with experiences that you will remember for the rest of your life. You will meet incredible people from diverse backgrounds, learn from world leading experts, and maybe even contribute original research to the world.

This book is a toolkit for you to use throughout your academic career. It will guide you through your teaching sessions, presentations, conferences, publications, and dissertations, and empower you to make the most of your university experience! Although this book contains the guidance you need to succeed academically, you may also encounter other tricky dilemmas during your time in higher education. You can always refer to this book to find sources of support and guidance. Every student will seek support at some point during their university journey, so it is not a sign of weakness. Remember, you deserve to thrive at university so allow yourself the tools and resources to succeed!

I hope you have a wonderful time at university!

Al the best

Charlotte

ACKNOWLEDGEMENTS

Thanks to the UniAdmissions team for offering me the opportunity to write this book, and the Senior Editor for their support throughout this writing journey.

I would also like to thank my family. I am extremely grateful for their hard work and support over the years, which have enabled me to seek education at the University of Oxford.

ABOUT UNIADMISSIONS

We currently publish over 100 titles across a range of subject areas – covering specialised admissions tests, examination techniques, personal statement guides, plus everything else you need to improve your chances of getting on to competitive courses and into competitive universities.

Outside of publishing we also operate a highly successful tuition division. This company was founded in 2013 by Dr Rohan Agarwal and Dr David Salt, both Cambridge Medical graduates with several years of tutoring experience. Since then, every year, hundreds of applicants and schools work with us on our programmes. Through the programmes we offer, we deliver expert tuition, exclusive course places, online courses, best-selling textbooks and much more.

With a team of over 500 Oxbridge tutors and a proven track record, UniAdmissions have quickly become the UK's number one admissions company.

Visit and engage with us at:

Website (UniAdmissions):www.uniadmissions.co.uk

Facebook:www.facebook.com/uniadmissionsuk

YOUR FREE BOOK

Thanks for purchasing this Ultimate Collection. Readers like you have the power to make or break a book –hopefully you found this one useful and informative. *UniAdmissions* would love to hear about your experiences with this book. As thanks for your time we'll send you another eBook from our Ultimate Guide series absolutely <u>FREE</u>!

★★★★★ ✓ Posted publicly as Amazon Customer | Clear

Write your review here

How to Redeem Your Free eBook

1) Find the book you have on your Amazon purchase history or your email receipt from other sites to help find the book online.

2) On the product page for the book, write your review and post it! Copy the review page or take a screen shot of the review you have left.

3) Head over to www.uniadmissions.co.uk/free-book and select your chosen free eBook!

Your eBook will then be emailed to you – it is as simple as that!